Reimagining the Christian Faith

Reimagining the Christian Faith

EXPLORING THE EMERGENT THEOLOGY OF DOUG PAGITT, PETER ROLLINS, SAMIR SELMANOVIC, & BRIAN MCLAREN

Jeremy Bouma

 THEOKLESIA

RENEW WEST MICHIGAN
Every purchase will help support
new West Michigan church plants.
Learn more at www.theoklesia.com/renew

Reimagining the Christian Faith: Exploring the Emergent Theology of Doug Pagitt,
Peter Rollins, Samir Selmanovic, & Brian McLaren

© 2012 by Jeremy Bouma

Published by **THEOKLESIA**
P.O. Box 1180
Grand Rapids, MI 49501
www.theoklesia.com

ISBN: 978-1-4783064-9-8

Printed in the United States of America

10 09 08 07 06 05 04 03 02 01

About **THEOKLESIA**

We are a hyperlocal idea curator dedicated to helping the Church of West Michigan rediscover the historic Christian faith for the 21st century. Jesus said that the Church is "the light of the world, a city on a hill that cannot be hidden." We provide the resources to help Her shine brightly in 21st century West Michigan by helping the Church connect God's Story of Rescue to our area, while remaining theologically rooted and biblically uncompromising.

www.theoklesia.com • info@theoklesia.com

CONTENT

INTRODUCTION

I remember the exact date when my journey toward taking Emergent theology to task began: August 2, 2008. It was the day my church hosted the *Church Basement Roadshow*, an innovative book tour featuring Emergent megastars Tony Jones, Doug Pagitt, and Mark Scandrette. Each of them released a new book that year that was instrumental in the ongoing Emergent effort to reimagine the Christian faith.

Because I was still thoroughly immersed in and connected to the Emergent Church movement, I jumped at the chance to host these Emergent heavyweights in my hometown and my church. I was so dedicated that I even donned red long johns—which I later found out to be pear-shaped Victoria's Secret lingerie—and a top-hat to play my part as the country bumpkin emcee.

Tony, Doug, and Mark didn't disappoint with a rousing performance of angsty post-evangelical faith-deconstruction ensconced in the garb of Grand Ole Opry showmanship. While most of my parishioners weren't in on the joke, there was a large contingent of post-everything Christians from the Grand Rapids area who positively lapped up their performance. Including a young high school graduate from my church who had been struggling with his faith.

I clearly remember the moment when I began moving toward taking Emergent theology to task, because I remember the moment when I saw this young high school graduate from my church walking around with a copy of Doug's new book, *A Christianity Worth Believing*, in tote.

You see, that summer I had read Doug's book and had begun to see some warning signs that things were not quite right with his theological enterprise. Th ere was a time I would have applauded his efforts at reimagining the Christian faith, and the fruit of that reimagination. But after a year of seminary I began to see cracks in the facade of Emergent's new kind of Christianity. I began to became increasingly uncomfortable with not only the deconstruction efforts of Emergent, but also their re-construction efforts. While that discomfort had not fully blossomed, it was there and I began to see the danger signs.

After reading Doug's book, I began to see the dangers the book and its theology posed. Yet, I invited Doug, Tony, and Mark, anyway. I hosted them and promoted them. And for selfish reasons: I wanted to be known as the guy who brought these three national authors and leaders to West Michigan; and I wanted to be known by these Emergent leaders so that I could, in someway, become an Emergent insider.

Lame, I know. Self-serving, really.

When I saw this young guy toting around Doug's book a tinge of regret washed over me—after I spent a graduate paper more closely examining Doug's theology, that tinge turned into full-on regret. I never did get around to talking to this young high school graduate about Doug's Christianity worth believing. After that experience, and subsequently examining Doug's book through the lens of historical theology, I began a journey toward taking the theology of the Emergent Church movement to task.

I also vowed I would never again trade my pastoral responsibility for stewarding theological truth for personal ambition or gain. Perhaps the past three years of writing in response to the Emergent Church has been a subconscious form of recompense for that August 2 moment—a sort of punishment-by-keyboard. Regardless, since that moment I have spent much of my academic career more closely examining the theology at root to the Emergent Church movement, the fruits of which are presented in this short book in a series of three essays, culled from my Master of Theology (ThM) program in historical theology.

The first essay came directly out of my August 2 experience. For a few years I had heard the charge that Doug Pagitt was a Pelagian, which was a not-so-subtle way of saying he was a heretic (Pelagianism is the heresy of Pelagius, a 5th century Church thinker condemned a heretic by the early church.) After reading his book I had a sense something was theologically off, and I wanted to see if Pagitt really was a Pelagian. So I spent a semester reading all of Pelagius' known letters and comparing his thoughts with Pagitt's. The result was an academic treatment of one of the Emergent Church's most vocal theological voices. That's the first essay, titled "Pagitt and Pelagius."

The second essay, "Rollins, Selmanovic, and Barth," came from a summer studying Karl Barth, the famous Swiss theologian often cited as a friend of Emergent. After reading four volumes of his massive *Church Dogmatics* I was struck by how little Barth actually has in common theologically with the Emergent Church. In fact, Barth would vociferously oppose much, if not most, Emergent theology for the same reasons he opposed liberal theology, particularly around the key doctrine of revelation. In this essay I revisited Emergent darling Peter Rollins and his book *How (Not) To Speak of God*, a pivotal book for my own Emergent predilections back in the day. After reading Barth I saw some problems with Rollins' hyper-transcendent view of God, and so I used Barth as a theological dialogue partner to respond to his views which seem to deny an actual revelation from God to humanity.

From there, I took a second prominent voice to task for his views of God's revelation outside of Jesus Christ: Samir Selmanovic. As the director of a prominent interfaith organization, Selmanovic is on the leading edges of the pluralism conversation within the Emergent Church. His views do not disappoint that leadership as he strongly suggests God's revelation isn't solely contained to Jesus Christ alone. Again, Barth has something to say about that, and I let him in theological dialogue with Selmanovic.

The final essay is reserved for the most prominent voice within Emergent, the so-called "grandfather"—or maybe it's "godfather"—of the Emergent Church movement: Brian McLaren. Love him or hate him, he is undeniably the most shaping voice in this movement, in many ways giving rise to it through his famous *New Kind of Christian* trilogy. For years, charges of theological liberalism were met with "he's just asking questions" dismissals. Th at changed in 2010, however, with the publication of *A New Kind of Christianity*, McLaren's theological opus that put to rest any questions that he and his friends were indeed reimagining the Christian faith.

But this reimagining effort wasn't in a way that was actually new and different. It was new and different to theologically ignorant evangelicals whom this reimagining enterprise was largely directed. McLaren's kind of Christianity is a very old kind of Christianity. About 200 years old, actually. His kind of Christianity is simply liberal Christianity repackaged for a new day.

Because I had heard for years the charge of liberalism leveled against McLaren, I wanted to see for myself if it was true, if he really was just a new kind of theological liberal. So one semester, during my course on the Modern Church in my Master of Th eology program, I read every English translation from one of the most prominent voices in historical theological liberalism: Albrect Ritschl. In this final essay, "McLaren and Ritschl," I show how McLaren follows footprint for footprint the path Ritschl tread long ago. How McLaren frames our problem, our solution, and the bearer of our solution are the ways in which liberalism has framed them for four generations. His is indeed an old kind of Christianity. (I should note that some of the content from McLaren's essay was revised and extended for a bigger work on historical theological liberalism that was published in May 2012: my Master's thesis, *Reimagining the*

Kingdom: The Generational Development of Liberal Kingdom Grammar from Schleiermacher to McLaren.)

If I have learned anything in the last few years at the end of my Th M program it's that theology matters. And when you get the pieces of theology wrong you ultimately get the gospel wrong. Of late, my generation is all a fl utter with reimagining the Christian faith—reimagining the pieces of the Christian faith. I understand this pull toward reimagining the Christian faith, because I have been there myself. What my generation needs, however, isn't to reimagine the Christian faith, but rediscover it. We need to rediscover what and how the Church of Jesus Christ has always believed about our problem, solution, and the One who bore that solution. We need to rediscover the gospel.

To be frank, that rediscovery effort is not going to come through the Emergent Church. As you will see through these short essays, it has become clear that their reimagination enterprise is simply one iteration in a long line of Protestant liberal leavers—Emergents have left the historic Christian faith in the same way liberals have every generation since Schleiermacher, yet in a way that's palatable for our postmodern, post-Christian day. Which, for this post-Emergent who had high hopes of a genuine third way that cuts through the malaise of contemporary liberal-conservative theologic discourse, is sad indeed.

I hope this short book will help expose some of the major theological thinkers in the Emergent Church movement for what they are: Purveyors and peddlers of recycled foreign theology other-than the historic Christian faith for a new, postmodern day. And I hope it will inspire some in the Church to take theology seriously and rediscover what the Church has always believed.

Reimagining the Christian Faith

Essay 1
Pagitt & Pelagius

Tony Jones, author and former National Coordinator of Emergent Village, wrote in a recent book, Th e New Christians, "We are not becoming less religious, as some people argue. We are becoming differently religious. And the shift is significant. Some call it a tectonic shift, others seismic or tsunamic. Whatever your geographical metaphor, the changes are shaking the earth beneath our feet." [1] Those changes include not only the shifting religious sentiments within the broad American religious landscape, but those within Protestantism itself. Specifically, a particular earth-shaking tectonic shift burst onto the stage

---

[1] Tony Jones, *The New Christians: Dispatches from the Emergent Frontier* (San Francisco: Jossey-Bass, 2008), 2.

of Evangelicalism nearly ten years ago in a "conversation" called Emergent. Over the last ten years books, conferences, and local conversations have given way to a national movement known as the Emerging Church. [2] In fact, one of its leaders, Brian McLaren, was named one of Time Magazine's 25 most influential evangelicals in America. [3] Consequently, many publishers now publish entire series of books by leading Emergent authors, in addition to the thousands of weblogs and community cohort meetings that drive local conversations. This conversation, then, is now a significant contemporary fixture in the broader evangelical community and national Christianity, making it necessary for the academy to take a serious examination of this movement's theology.

The Emerging Church was born out of a need to both contextually engage our shifting postmodern culture with the teachings, way, and person of Jesus Christ, and rethink traditional doctrines of the Church. Th us, this movement within Evangelicalism is both missional and theological. It is the second facet with which many have taken issue. In true postmodern form, it appears that nothing is off the table when it comes to the in-vogue postmodern deconstructive process: penal substitutionary atonement is

---

[2] Two terms need clarification at the beginning: 1) Emergent (also known as Emergent Village) is the national 501(c)3 nonprofit organization that acts as a coordinating 'hub' for 2) the Emerging Church, a broader movement within mostly evangelicalism to rethink Christian Spirituality both missionally and theologically in light of postmodernism. I will use the two terms in these separate forms to delineate between the broad conversation and a specific organization.

[3] "25 Most Influential Evangelicals In America," *Time Magazine*, February 7, 2005.

altogether dismissed as "divine child abuse;" [4] the apostle John's testimony regarding the need to "believe in" Jesus is replaced with an "opt-out" program of universal inclusivism; [5] and a Grand Rapids pastor frequently insists that "as far as we know the tomb is empty." [6] While their penchant for dialogue over church, spirituality, and theology is appreciated—we certainly should not shy away from re-thinking and re-learning theology—the question remains, however, at what point is this conversation no longer Christian?

One of the most significant facets of Emerging Church theology that pushes the limits of the (non)Christian conversational label is its perspective on human nature after the Fall. Jones himself represents a growing consensus within this conversation that rejects the historic doctrine of original sin. He suggests that nothing in the biblical account of creation or Paul's examination of human nature suggests a change at the genetic, fundamental level nor is a tainted spiritual nature passed from mother to child biologically. [7] He goes so far as to suggest the Apostle Paul was wrong about human nature in Romans 5 and rejects original sin altogether, insisting that this doctrine is

---

[4] Brian McLaren, *The Story We Find Ourselves In* (San Francisco: Jossy-Bass, 2003) 102.

[5] See Spencer Burke, *A Heretic's Guide to Eternity* (San Francisco: Jossey-Bass, 2006).

[6] While Rob Bell, pastor of Mars Hill Bible Church, may not himself deny the bodily resurrection of Jesus Christ, this statement certainly leaves open the possibility that the tomb might, for all we know, *not* be empty.

[7] While Rob Bell, pastor of Mars Hill Bible Church, may not himself deny the bodily resurrection of Jesus Christ, this statement certainly leaves open the possibility that the tomb might, for all we know, *not* be empty.

"neither biblically, philosophically, nor scientifically tenable." [8]   Clearly, a national deconstructive effort is underway to re-define a doctrine that has been part of historic Christian orthodoxy for centuries. No one within the Emerging Church has come as close, however, to setting forth an alternative to this historic Christian doctrine than pastor and emergent leader Doug Pagitt.

Pagitt is the founding and teaching pastor of an emerging church community outside Minneapolis, Minnesota called Solomon's Porch. Aside from his duties as teaching pastor for his church, Pagitt has helped navigate and position Emergent as an alternative to existing, traditional versions of Christianity through radio interviews, conferences, blogs, and books. Last year, Pagitt solidified those navigation and positioning efforts with his theological opus, A Christianity Worth Believing. In the book's opening page, Pagitt sets forth the purpose for writing his book:

> I don't believe in the versions of Christianity that have prevailed for the last fifteen hundred years, the ones that were perfectly suitable for their time and place but have little connection with this time and place. The ones that answer questions we no longer ask and fail to consider questions we can no longer ignore. The ones that don't mesh with what we know about God

---

[8] Tony Jones, *Original Sin: A Depraved Idea*, 26 January, 2009. http://blog.beliefnet.com/tonyjones/2009/01/original-sin-a-depraved-idea.html and *Was Paul Wrong?* 18 February, 2009, http://blog.beliefnet.com/tonyjones/2009/02/was-paul-wrong.html.

and the world and our place in it...I am
conflicted because I want to believe differently. [9]

While Pagitt may believe he is believing differently—
and consequently believe he is offering the world a
different Christianity that is more believable than the
current form—in reality he is simply believing *otherly*; the
form of Christianity that Pagitt pushes is neither innovative
nor different: it is a form of Christianity other-than the
versions that *currently* exist but mirrors those that have
already existed. Whether by intention or accident, the
Christian faith that Pagitt believes "feels alive, sustainable,
and meaningful in *our* day" [10] is really a form of faith from
an *other* day. Th is paper examines that other faith and
theology of Pagitt in relation to two thinkers from that
other day (the late early church), Pelagius and Augustine.
In true postmodern, Emergent form, Pelagius and
Augustine will act as theological dialogue partners with
this contemporary self-proclaimed theologian in order to
assess his theology on human nature and sin, and the
consequences of those thoughts for the gospel. While Pagitt
may conclude that a person does not "have to be a fifth-
century Augustinian in order to be a follower of Jesus," [11]
our study will reveals how closely Pagitt resembles an other
belief from the same period of time: the beliefs of Pelagius.
From his view of human nature and sin, salvation,

---

[9] Doug Pagitt, *A Christianity Worth Believing* (San Francisco: Jossey-Bass, 2008), 2.

[10] Pagitt, *Christianity*, xii. (Emphasis mine).

[11] Pagitt, *Christianity*, 49.

discipleship, and judgment, this paper explores how Pagitt mirrors the theology of Pelagius, while describes the responses of Augustine to Pelagius as a means of responding to Pagitt today.

While Pagitt rejects the versions of Christianity that have prevailed, he resurrects an other form of Christianity from the past that was deemed a threat to the gospel: Pelagianism. In the story of Christian theology, the 5th century is known mostly for the doctrinal dispute between Pelagius of Britain and Augustine of Hippo. The controversy stemmed largely from the differing concepts of humanity's relation to God which both men had been preaching for a generation. [12] Pelagius' outlook regarding human nature was the opposite of Augustine's: the trouble was not nature, but habit, thus every person is responsible for his or her own sin, not because Adam infected the human race. [13] Led by Augustine, Pelagius' opponents charged him and his followers with three things: 1) denying original sin; 2) denying God's grace as essential for salvation; and 3) preaching sinless perfection through free will apart from grace. [14] For the next twenty years, the two would argue over the the nature of humanity post-fall, the nature of sin, the ability to be sinless through personal effort, and the role of grace in the life of a person. Ultimately, however, the battle was over the nature of salvation itself. As Roger Olson says, "The story of

---

[12] W. C. Frend, *The Rise of Christianity* (Philadelphia: Fortress Press, 1984.), 675.

[13] Frend, *Rise of Christianity*, 674.

[14] Roger E. Olson, *The Story of Christian Theology* (Downers Grove, IL: IVP Academic, 1999), 269.

Christian theology is the story of Christian reflection on salvation." [15] The same is true today.

As the Emerging Church has grown in prominence, some have begun to label it a "conversation of heresy," especially a conversation steeped in the so-called Pelagian heresy. Likewise, some have charged Pagitt with the so-called heresy of Pelagianism. Therefore, because the Emerging Church is becoming a dominant alternative within broader Evangelicalism it is important to understand the significance of this movement's theology. Furthermore, because Pagitt is a significant leader and thinker within the Emerging Church, it behooves the academy to examine how his "hope-filled, open-armed, alive-and-well-faith for the left out, left behind, and let down in us all" [16] is a repackaged previously existing version of Christian spirituality. In the end, interacting with Pagitt's, Pelagius', and Augustine's works will reveal that Pagitt embraces an other form of faith that both the Communion of Saints and Spirit of God have deemed foreign to the Holy Scriptures, Rule of Faith, and gospel of Jesus Christ.

HUMAN NATURE & SIN

Like Pelagius, it appears that Pagitt has reacted to Augustinian theology. For Pagitt, Augustine's doctrine of depravity was based on cultural readings and understandings of certain biblical passages; the doctrine of

---

[15] Olson, *Christian Theology*, 13.

[16] The subtitle to Pagitt's book.

original sin isn't biblical, it is cultural. [17] In fact, after citing sections from the Westminster Confession of Faith, Augsburg Confession, and *Book of Common Prayer* on Original Sin, Pagitt asserts that these "versions" as "extreme theology" that do not fit the Christian story. [18] The starting point for these confessions and explanations of human nature flow from a source (Augustinian theology) that started with a view of humanity born out of a Greco-Roman world that centered on dualism and separation from God.

According to Pagitt, this theology could not reconcile its assumptions of human frailty and limitations with the story from the Scriptures that said humans were created in the image of God. "So the theology of depravity made sense to people who held a view of humans as being something less than God had intended." [19] For Pagitt, original sin was a cultural response to a wrongly held assumption that the current condition of humanity was less than the condition at which they were originally created. This false assumption about the starting place of human nature led to a "false doctrine" on how human nature is now, later resulting in distortions of the doctrine of salvation and judgment. Pagitt believes "the rationale for this view of humanity has expired, and so ought the theology that grew out of it." [20] Because Augustinian theology begins with the false assumption that humans are

---

[17] Pagitt, *Christianity*, 127.

[18] Pagitt, *Christianity*, 123-124.

[19] Pagitt, *Christianity*, 128.

[20] Pagitt, *Christianity*, 128.

now, post-Fall, different than they were intended at Creation, the Church should abandon it.

Pagitt insists we need to tell a better story, a story (read: theology) that explains we are still created in the unbroken Image of God as partners and collaborators with Him who are still His people; this story never loses "sight of what it means to be created in the Image of God." [21]   The Imago Dei plays a central role in Pagitt's theology of human nature. He insists that the story of God says the Imago Dei is the same as it ever was. While we were created to partner with God as Images of God, we still are; the Image of God has not changed. Most Christians who hold to the historic belief of the doctrine of the Imago Dei believe that image is cracked, broken, and tainted at some level. Pagitt, however, believes nothing has inherently changed about that Image —about human nature—from the very beginning of Creation. Referencing the Genesis 3 narrative of Adam and Eve, Pagitt says, "Their state of being did not change, their DNA didn't change...This story never suggests that the sin of Adam and Eve sends them into a state of depravity." [22] In fact, "we are still capable of living as children of God" because we can still regard human nature as being "inherently godly." [23]   Th is strong belief in the original Imago Dei plays strongly into Pagitt's belief in the fundamental goodness of humanity and capacity to choose good over evil.

---

[21] Pagitt, *Christianity*, 129-130.

[22] Pagitt, *Christianity*, 129-130.

[23] Pagitt, *Christianity*, 136, 137.

Taking his cues from Celtic Christians, Pagitt believes that all humans "posses the light of God within them. That light might brighten or dim as a person lives well with God or moves away from God, but the light is never extinguished." [24] The chief end of humanity isn't to simply glorify God, as the Westminster Confession suggests, but to "*live* like God," [25] a capacity Pagitt believes is inherent within our nature. It is clear that for Pagitt, we are still good and can still choose to live godly. Nothing changed within human nature because of Adam, we are still the way we intended, though "we are invited to live free from sin and destruction, to seek lives lived in harmony with God." [26] But as Pagitt asks, if we are not born sinners, why do we sin? If we are still born as we were intended to be at Creation, why don't we live "in harmony with God?"

Instead of starting out rotten, "the systems, hurts, and patterns of this world create disharmony with God and one another. It is life that creates illness and sin." [27] While we are born good and godly, examples, habits, and ignorance from our life taint our in-born goodness. Pagitt offers an example of a newborn baby to argue his case. In the case of a newborn, we should not view him or her as full of evil, but instead should understand that this newborn begins life entirely good. That good child is affected, trained, and drawn into sin because of the examples other sin-trained models provide. Children sin because they practice what is

---

[24] Pagitt, *Christianity*, 141, 142.

[25] Pagitt, *Christianity*, 143. Emphasis mine.

[26] Pagitt, *Christianity*, 160.

[27] Pagitt, *Christianity*, 165.

modeled for them by adults or older siblings, continue in those practices and form habits, and simply do not know better.[28]   Sin manifests itself and affects people from the outside in, rather than the inside out; our nature is not broken, but our examples, habits, and knowledge are.

But as Pagitt suggests, "when sin is active, we must deal with it; the good news is we can."[29]   Because we were created good, and still are, we are invited and capable of living free from sin and destruction, to seek to live in harmony with God. Pagitt goes further by suggesting, "We can live lives in a collective way, so the systems that cause disharmony with God can be changed. We can change the patterns wired into us from our families and create new ways of relating and being. In other words, we can be born-again, new creations."[30]   While the implications of this quotation for salvation and the Gospel will be addressed later, what is clear is that Pagitt believes that humans on their own can change, in their own power; by themselves they can become new creations. During this discourse on changing and being "born-again," Pagitt mentions neither the power of Christ nor the presence of the Holy Spirit. Instead, when sin comes to tempt us, *we* are the ones who flee from, plot against, and eradicate it.[31]   In other words, people can by *nature*, through their own inner capacity, choose to be "in sync" or "out of sync" with God. Th ey themselves challenge and change the systems and patterns

---

[28] See Pagitt, *Christianity*, 165 for the author's complete illustration.

[29] Pagitt, *Christianity*, 163.

[30] Pagitt, *Christianity*, 167. (Emphasis mine).

[31] Pagitt, *Christianity*, 164.

which impinge upon their still-intact Imago Dei. Th ese ideas on human nature and sin are not merely different than current versions of Christianity, they simply mirror an *other*. That other is Pelagius.

Like Pagitt, Pelagius begins with anthropology. His view of human nature can be summarized by a section from his letter *On Chastity*:

> Reflect carefully then, I beg you, on the good which is yours if you always remain such as God created man from the beginning and as he sent him forth thereafter, when he had brought him into the world. Observe what a blessing it is to be always in the state in which you were created and to preserve the features of your first birth. For no one is born corrupt nor is anyone stained by corruption before the lapse of an appointed period of time. Every man is seen to posses among his initial attributes what was there at the beginning, so that he has no excuse thereafter if he loses through his own negligence what he possessed by nature. [32]

For Pelagius, the original Imago Dei has not changed; God created humans good and uncorrupt, and they still exist in this good, uncorrupted state. We are to remain and live out of the originally created good nature by pursuing the virtues of God. Like Pagitt, Pelagius places great emphasis on the original Image of God after which humans were (and still are) fashioned together. We are still to

---

[32] Pelagius. "On Chastity," from *The Letters of Pelagius and His Followers*, ed. by B. R. Rees. (Suffolk, England: The Boydell Press, 1991), 259. (Emphasis mine).

measure the good of human nature by reference to its Creator, supposing He has made people exceedingly good.[33] Pelagius (like Pagitt) reacted to any notion that humanity was corrupt and incapable of choosing to follow the commands of God.

Pelagius believed that God bestowed on His rational human creatures the gift of "doing good out of (the creature's) own free will and capacity to exercise free choice." [34] God the Creator gave humans the inner capacity to do good or evil. Even now we can choose to do either out of our natural capacity and ability. Embedded within us is a "natural sanctity in our minds which administers justice equally on the evil and the good and...distinguishes the one side from the other by a kind of inner law."[35] Using this inner capacity, natural sanctity, and inner law, humans are naturally capable of living "in sync with God" or "out of sync with God," to choose honorable and upright actions or wrong deeds. The reason people can live *in* or *out* of sync with God is because nature does not determine their ability to do so; this "living" is a product of choice. As Pelagius argues, "When will a man guilty of any crime or sin accept with a tranquil mind that his wickedness is a product of his own will, not of necessity, and allow what he now strives to attribute to nature to be ascribed to his own free choice?"[36]

---

[33] B. R. Rees. "To Demetrias," from *The Letters of Pelagius and His Followers.* (Suffolk, England: The Boydell Press, 1991), 37.

[34] Pelagius, "To Demetrias," 38.

[35] Pelagius, "To Demetrias," 40.

[36] Pelagius. "On the Possibility of Not Sinning," from *The Letters of Pelagius and His Followers.* Ed. B. R. Rees. (Suffolk, England: The Boydell Press, 1991), 167-168.

In fact, it is God himself who presupposes our unfettered inner ability to choose good or evil. According to Pelagius' logic, if God has commanded us to love God and love people—if God has commanded us not to sin—then we must by nature have the capacity to choose good. "No one knows better the true measure of our strength than He who has given it to us nor does anyone understand better how much we are able to do than He who has given us this very capacity of ours to be able; nor has He who is just wished to command anything impossible or He who is good intended to condemn a man for doing what he could not avoid." [37] In typical Pelagian form, he insists that if humans are naturally incapable of being without sin, then there would be no command to be holy. Consequently, if God commanded us to be good, then we must be able to choose good; if we are able to choose good, then we must able to do good. Because God created us good we are good and are capable of doing good.

How then would Pelagius answer Pagitt's question, "Why do we sin?" We sin for three reasons: examples, habits, and ignorance. Both Pagitt and Pelagius view human nature as fundamentally flawless, still good even post-Fall. No one has a corrupted nature. Pelagius defended the goodness of nature and ability to choose either goodness or wickedness. In his letter *To Demetrias*, Pelagius declares that our nature is capable of doing good and evil and that he wants to "protect it from an unjust charge, so that we may not seem to be forced to do evil

---

[37] Pelagius, "To Demetrias," 53-54.

through a fault in our nature." [38] Pelagius insists we do things by choice through the exercise of our will, and he wants to make sure that we are not forced to do evil but have the freedom to choose. He doesn't want anything to stand in the way of our will's ability to choose good or evil. Sinning is the product of our will, not of necessity of nature. [39] If this is true, if our nature is good, why then do we sin? For Pelagius, the answer begins with Adam.

Pelagius makes clear that "through Adam sin came at a time when it did not yet exist...through the former's sin (Adam's) death came in; Adam is the source of sin." [40] Adam is the archetype not only for sin, but also for sinning. He was the fi rst example of disobedience that later influenced generations into sinning. [41] In fact, "all are condemned for following his example." [42] From Adam's pattern and example of disobedience, his descendants modeled for others what Adam modeled for them. Since then, generations of humans have perpetuated that original pattern for disobedience, which has petrified into habits of sin; patterns has led to habits.

In his letters and commentary, it is clear Pelagius believes generations of humans have been "instructed" and "educated in evil." We possess a "long habit of doing wrong

---

[38] Pelagius, "To Demetrias," 43.

[39] Pelagius, "On the Possibility of Not Sinning," 167-168.

[40] Pelagius, *Romans*, 92, 93.

[41] Pelagius, *Romans*, 95.

[42] Pelagius. "On the Christian Life," from *The Letters of Pelagius and His Followers*. Ed. B. R. Rees (Suffolk, England: The Boydell Press, 1991), 121.

which has infected us from childhood and corrupted us little by little over many years and ever after holds us in bondage and slavery to itself, so that it seems somehow to have acquired the force of nature." [43]   While nature is not corrupt, the example set by Adam and subsequent generations has formed corrupting habits. Now, humans are "drunk with the habit of sins" so that we do not know what we do. [44]   In commenting on Romans 7:17 and the "Sin that lives in me," Pelagius says, "[Sin] lives as a guest and as one thing in another, not as one single thing; in other words, as an accidental quality, not a natural one." [45] Our sin is not natural, it is accidental because of the "guest of habit" that has formed within all of us. As Pagitt suggests, we are influenced by systems that model for us disintegration and patterns that are wired into us by others. In the end, Pelagius exclaims, "I who am held prisoner in this way—who will set me free from this fatal, corporeal habit?" [46]

Not only has the example of Adam and others influenced us and our habits, ignorance has, too. "The thick fog of folly and ignorance has so blinded our mind that it is incapable of feeling or saying anything divinely inspired." [47] Over time, human reason and nature has been "buried beneath an excess of vices" because of a "long habituation

---

[43] Pelagius, "To Demetrias," 44.

[44] Pelagius, *Romans*, 104.

[45] Pelagius, *Romans*, 104.

[46] Pelagius, *Romans*, 105.

[47] Pelagius, "To Demetrias," 45.

of sinning," and is "tainted with the rust of ignorance." [48] We no longer know what we are doing, because we are ignorant about what we should be doing. Though Pelagius does not go into detail about how we become ignorant or from where this ignorance comes, it makes sense it would arise from the confusion which disobedient examples and patterns cause and the habits that are formed from following those disobedient patterns. Ignorance, then, comes from the foreign example of Adam and others and both arises from and influences our habits. Through our freedom of choice, we respond to the example of Adam and others, leading to the formation of habits and ignorance of correct living. Now out of ignorance and habit we host the "guest of sin" and live as if drunk on those perpetual carnal habits. While Pelagius still believes we are responsible to choose righteously, examples, ignorance, and poor habits impinge upon our natural ability to choose.

In summation, neither Pagitt nor Pelagius believe anyone is born corrupt or stained by corruption. They both appeal to the original Imago Dei and the Creator as a defense for this belief. They believe God made us as good Image Bearers and our sin doesn't change this good nature. Both insist that our inner nature (and according to Pagitt, our DNA) did not change after the Fall; we still posses God's spark of godliness within us. Instead of the necessity of nature forcing us to sin, Pelagius and Pagitt insist that we sin when we follow the example of Adam and others into living lives of disintegration from God. Following those patterns, habits formed out of doing wrong from childhood have corrupted us to the point that sin inhabits our lives as

---

[48] Rees, "To Demetrias," 44.

a guest to the point we are drunk on those habits of sin. Sin is not natural, but accidental. Through bad examples and habits, we have been educated in ignorance, so that we now do not know what we do nor what we should do. In the end, both Pelagius and Pagitt believe we are not born depraved and nothing internal causes us to sin. Instead, systems, patterns, and habits outside of us lead us into living lives of disharmony with God and one another. The good news, according to both, is that we can change these patterns and live out of our natural good capacity. Pelagius' and Pagitt's theology of humanity and sin have great bearing on another, greater theology: the theology of salvation.

SALVATION, DISCIPLESHIP, & JUDGMENT

Pagitt, like much of the Emerging Church, rejects penal substitutionary atonement as a framing narrative for understanding humanity's reconciliation with God. Instead, he supplies what might be considered a moral example theory of atonement, though he rejects any atonement theory and would cringe at such a comparison. Because human nature is fundamentally godly and merely impinged upon by broken, sinful systems, humanity can be saved merely by following a better example. Since humans have the inner, natural capacity to do good or evil, their salvation comes not through a sacrifice but through a new model and set of teachings by which they can know how to act and form new habits. Consequently, the life, Way, pattern, and teachings of Jesus are the center of Emerging Church theology and form the core of Pagitt's views on salvation, too.

Broadly speaking, Pagitt believes Jesus came to call people to join in with God, rather than the systems of disintegration. Pagitt writes concerning the early Christians: "The Messiah was their map, their guide to what true partnership with God looked like" through His example and teachings; Jesus "restored them to the lives for which they were created."[49] Salvation comes, then, when people "follow Jesus as Joshua into the promised land of freedom and release," because he is the new pattern of harmony for humanity by showing us what full integration with God looks like and fulfilling what people are meant to do and be.[50] According to Pagitt, the problem is not that humanity is depraved, that human nature is marked and tainted by sin which causes people to sin. Instead, human nature is marked and defined by a sound *Imago Dei* that carries with it the capacity to choose integration with God or disintegration from God. Sinful choices from the outside, through sinful systems and patterns, influence that sound Image into forming ongoing habits, which lead to ongoing sin. What humanity requires, then, is someone to model for us integration with God, to show us a better more *original* way of being human. Jesus is that person. As Pagitt argues, "He tells his followers, *shows* his followers, what it looks like to live in harmony with God. Because Jesus is the Son of God, he is the *very model* of complete integration with the Creator. And because Jesus is the Son of humanity, he is the *very model* of living out that integration in the midst of war, pain, joy, conflict, love, loss,

---

[49] Rees, "To Demetrias," 44.

[50] Pagitt, *Christianity*, 182, 208.

and fear." [51]   According to Pagitt, then, humanity has corrupt, sin-tainted patterns that model sin and influence sin-formed habits.

Salvation, then, comes not through a sacrifice that does something with the objective, natural realities of rebellion, evil, and death. [52]   Instead,   salvation comes through an example, a new pattern that models for us integration with God. For Pagitt, the cross was not about the suffering, bloodshed, and death of Jesus, for that was the old "Greek blood god" version of atonement. [53]   Instead, "Jesus is the core of Christianity because it is through Jesus that we see the fullness of God's hopes for the world. Jesus is the redemption of the creation plan. He *shows* us what is means to live in partnership with our creator. He *leads* us into what it means to be integrated with God." [54]   Salvation is found in the example and model that Jesus shows humanity; we find redemption through the the leadership of Jesus into better patterns and better habits that are integrated with God. Because human nature is untainted and still intact, we merely need a better model than the one that failed us before. Th us, Jesus is a new Adam for creation, a new example and model. For Pagitt, "Just as

---

[51] Pagitt, *Christianity*, 182, 208.

[52] As evidenced in the previous section, humanity does not possess a sin-tainted nature; our "DNA hasn't changed." Instead, examples, patterns, and systems press against our will, influencing our choices and forming sin habits.

[53] Pagitt, *Christianity*, 194.

[54] Pagitt, *Christianity*, 195.

Adam was the pattern of disobedience, so Jesus is the new pattern of harmony." [55]

Interestingly, Pelagius in his commentary on Romans translates "pattern" as "type" and offers this commentary: "Adam is the source of sin, so too is Christ the source of righteousness." Elsewhere in commentary on 5:12, Pelagius says that sin came into the world "by example or by pattern." And in 5:19 he says, "Just as by the example of Adam's disobedience many sinned, so also many are justified by Christ's obedience." [56] Clearly, Pagitt mirrors Pelagius' contrast between the example/pattern of Adam's disobedience vs. the example/pattern of obedience, or "harmony" to use Pagitt's language. Because of the disobedient example of Adam, "generations of disintegration" followed his pattern and developed habits of disintegration. Jesus came to provide a new, better model after which new generations of humans could pattern their lives, developing habits of "integration with the Creator." Salvation is found in the example, model, and pattern of Jesus Christ, not His suffering, bloodshed, and death on a cross.

---

[55] Pagitt, *Christianity*, 208. Interestingly, Pelagius in his commentary on Romans translates "pattern" as "type" and offers this commentary: "Adam is the source of sin, so too is Christ the source of righteousness." Elsewhere in commentary on 5:12, Pelagius says that sin came into the world "by example or by pattern." And in 5:19 he says, "Just as by the example of Adam's disobedience many sinned, so also many are justified by Christ's obedience." Pelagius, *Romans*, 92-95. Clearly, Pagitt mirrors Pelagius' contrast between the example/pattern of Adam's disobedience vs. the example/pattern of obedience, or "harmony" to use Pagitt's language.

[56] Pelagius, *Romans*, 92-95.

This theology of "salvation by example" influences how Pagitt views discipleship and eschatology. Those who decide to follow this new pattern are invited into God's work now, for "the kingdom-of-God gospel calls us to partner with God, to be full participants in the life God is creating, to follow in the way of Jesus as we seek to live as people who are fully integrated with our Creator." [57] Instead of choosing to live lives of disintegration, we are called to be fully integrated with God now. This is possible because 1) we are "inherently godly," having the "light of God" within us; and 2) "we can change the patterns wired into us from our families and create new ways of relating and being." [58] Discipleship, then, is about choosing to live well with God in this life.

The problem comes when the question, "Why?" is asked. Why must we live lives of integration? Pagitt does not address judgment or what happens when one does not choose to live a life of integration with God, or better put, when a person intentionally chooses not to "partner with God" or seek to live as a person who is fully integrated with their Creator. Instead, Pagitt assures the world that "God will dwell among us, that God will be with us, that the whole of creation will be healed and restored and fully integrated with God. Earthly life will be made new as it is transformed into the Kingdom of God." [59]   While Pagitt reflects Pelagius in calling people to find salvation and life in the example of Jesus and calls all people to follow Jesus'

---

[57] Pagitt, *Christianity*, 226.

[58] Pagitt, *Christianity*, 137, 141, 167.

[59] Pagitt, *Christianity*, 230-231.

pattern of integration with God, he does not go as far as Pelagius does soteriologically and eschatologically.

Pelagius both reflects and contrasts Pagitt's theology of salvation. Like Pagitt, Pelagius looks to Christ as a new example and model. In *On the Christian Life*, Pelagius says, "let no man judge himself to be a Christian, unless he is one who both follows the teachings of Christ and imitates His example."[60] Elsewhere he says, "Men are not Christians unless they follow the pattern and teaching of Christ. A Christian is one who lives by Christ's example."[61] In his commentary on Romans Pelagius says Christ "offered, by way of grace to overcome sin, *teaching and example*."[62] While a Christian is certainly called to follow the example of Jesus and live out his teachings—no person can be called a Christian unless they both believe in Christ and live in Him through obedience—this emphasis on the teachings and example of Christ makes more sense when Pelagius' view of salvation comes into focus.

For Pelagius, the teachings and example of Christ are of utmost importance to ensure salvation in the end. A person is forgiven of sins and becomes a Christian initially at baptism. Baptism is the event at which a person becomes a son or daughter of God and is reborn.[63] A person believes with his heart and is justified and he confesses with his lips

---

[60] Rees, "On the Christian Life," 123.

[61] Pelagius. "To an Old Friend," from *The Letters of Pelagius and His Followers*. Ed. by B. R. Rees (Suffolk, England: The Boydell Press, 1991), 151.

[62] Pelagius, *Romans*, 98. Emphasis mine.

[63] Pelagius, "To Demetrias," 56.

and is saved, all of which is fulfilled at baptism when sins are washed away. [64]   Forgiveness and justification, then, happens during baptism, but for past sins. This is clear from Pelagius' letter, *On Bad Teachers*: "Faith is an aid in ridding us of sin...that is to say, it releases us from sins already committed but does not grant pardon and immunity for those which we commit in the future." [65] People come to Christ by faith and find forgiveness for sins committed thus far through baptism, but not for sins committed afterwards. "If there is to be sinning thereafter, what does it profit us to have washed it away?" [66]   Here Pelagius warns Christians not to sin after they have received the forgiveness of sins and justification through baptism. In fact, he goes so far to say "If you sin [in the future], you will not be under grace." [67]   According to Pelagius, in order not to sin into the future, post-baptism we need the example of Christ.

Unlike Pagitt—who's soteriology does not incorporate suffering and bloodshed, believing "Jesus was not sent as the selected one to appease the anger of the Greek blood god" [68] —Pelagius actually believes Christ carried our sins and suffered for us to provide justification, forgiveness, and freedom from future sin. This suffering and death on the

---

[64] Pelagius, "On the Christian Life," 122.

[65] Pelagius. "On Bad Teachers," from *The Letters of Pelagius and His Followers*. Ed. by B. R. Rees (Suffolk, England: The Boydell Press, 1991), 217.

[66] Pelagius, "On the Christian Life," 122.

[67] Pelagius, *Romans*, 99.

[68] Pagitt, *Christianity*, 194.

cross provides forgiveness from past sins and releases us from being "drunk with the habit of sin" [69] so that we can follow the example of Christ and choose not to sin. In his analysis of Romans 5:10 Pelagius says, "If we have been saved by Christ's death, how much more shall we glory in his life, if we imitate it!" [70] Furthermore, in 5:11 he writes, "[Paul] means to show that Christ suffered so that we who had forsaken God by following Adam might be reconciled to God through Christ." [71] Finally, in 5:12 Pelagius says:

> *"Therefore just as through one person sin came into the world, and through sin death. By example, or by pattern. Just as through Adam sin came at a time when it did not yet exist, so in the same way through Christ righteousness was recovered at a time when it survived in almost no one. And just as through the former's sin death came in, so also through the later's righteousness life was regained."* [72]

The context of all three verses is examples and patterns. Since humanity fell into sin through the example of Adam and formed habits of sin based on his pattern, we need a new example and a new pattern after baptism in order not to sin in the future. Christ, then, is compared to the

---

[69] Pelagius, *Romans*, 102. In reference to Rom. 7:15, Pelagius says that we on our own accord after subjecting ourselves to sin and the habit of sin act as if "drunk with the habit of sin," so that we do not know what we do.

[70] Pelagius, *Romans*, 92.

[71] Pelagius, *Romans*, 92.

[72] Pelagius, *Romans*, 92.

example of Adam. While sin came through the example of Adam, righteousness was recovered through His example; whereas through the example of Adam's sin death arrived, through the example of Christ's righteousness life was regained. Even though the event of the cross—an event that somewhat mirrors Reformed expressions of penal substitutionary atonement—was the catalyst for forgiveness, it seems to be the example of Christ that actually provides for life, eternal life.

Although Pelagius doesn't explicitly articulate it, it seems that he believes salvation occurs by following the example of Christ. Unfortunately, the depth of understanding of Pelagius' soteriology pales in comparison to our understanding of his anthropology and hamartiology. Considering how important the example of Adam and subsequent generations of humans are to influencing human nature to sin, however, it seems plausible that the example of Christ would provide the needed antidote to humanity's sin-drunk habit. While "Christ has redeemed us with His blood from death" and actually Himself conquered death in the process, if we stop sinning only then will our redemption be profitable.[73] We are redeemed and forgiven through his death from past sins, but attain the profit of that redemption in the future (eternal life) by stopping our habit of sinning. Pelagius makes this clear in his letter *On the Christian Life* when he says, "How can [a person] hope for everlasting life from God, if he has not earned it by good deeds...whoever has not been good has not life; whoever has not performed works of righteousness and mercy cannot reign with

---

[73] Pelagius, *Romans*, 82.

Christ." [74] This makes more sense when one realizes that Pelagius believes both faith and deeds are important.

While Pagitt mirrors Pelagius' theology of the example of Christ for attaining (eternal) life, Pelagius contrasts with Pagitt by insisting that faith is also required. Throughout his book, Pagitt never says that faith is required for the forgiveness of sins and salvation. Instead, "the way to God is to walk the path Jesus walked, the path of obedience, of integration, of partnership." [75]   Unlike Pagitt, Pelagius believes that faith is important, but not faith alone. In his commentary on Romans 3:28 Pelagius indicates that a person in coming to Christ is saved when he first believes by faith. [76] Elsewhere Pelagius said we are saved by Christ's death and are forgiven of our sins by Christ. As he says in his letter *On the Christian Life*, "the faith of all holds that sins are washed away by baptism," which occurs when someone believes in his heart and confesses with his lips. [77] Presumably, Pelagius holds that a person believes in Jesus' redemption for sins and defeat of death through the cross when he comes by faith to be cleansed of his sins through baptism. At the moment of baptism, belief, confession and faith leads to justification, salvation, and forgiveness. [78]

Unlike Pagitt, Pelagius believes a person first finds new life through faith. Pelagius does not believe, however, that a

---

[74] Rees, "On the Christian Life," 117.

[75] Pagitt, *Christianity*, 211.

[76] Pelagius, *Romans,* 83.

[77] Rees, "On the Christian Life," 122.

[78] To understand all the "pieces" of this argumentation, see Rees, *The Letters*, 117, Pelagius, *Romans,* 82.

person can have hope in faith alone. "So, if a man sins after gaining faith and receiving the holy lather (baptism), let him no longer hope for pardon through faith alone, as he did before baptism, but let him rather entreat it with weeping and wailing, with abstinence and fasting, even with sackcloth and ashes, and all manner of lamentation."[79] After a person receives baptism and sins, she can no longer hope that the faith that brought her to baptism and belief in Christ to begin with will pardon her for those future sins; faith alone does not pardon for sins committed after the initial event of faith (read: baptism). In *On the Christian Life*, Pelagius argues, "For if faith alone is required, it is superfluous to order the commandments be kept." Since God has commanded people to keep his commandments, Pelagius surmises that eternal life is gained by both faith and deeds. Unless a person follows the example of Christ post-baptism, unless he chooses to keep the commands of Christ he has not life and will not share life with Christ." [80]

Perhaps this is why Pelagius places such a premium on discipleship and takes judgment seriously. In *To Demetrias* he says, "The bride of Christ must be more splendidly adorned than anything else, since the greater one whom one is seeking to please the greater the effort which is required to please him." [81] The bride is called to live a life that is "blameless" and "guiltless" in order to reign with Christ in the end, "for nothing is worthier of God, nothing

---

[79] Rees, "On Bad Teachers," 217. (Emphasis mine).

[80] Rees, "On the Christian Life," 123.

[81] Rees, "To Demitrias," 123.

can be more dear to him, than the blamelessness should be maintained with all possible circumspect." [82] Why? What is the promise for those who fail to live such a life post-baptism? Judgment and hell. Pelagius makes plain in On Divine Law that those who believe in Christ and receive him through baptism and renounce the devil and the world are called to pay attention to the things which are forbidden and to diligently fulfill the things commanded, because "the punishment of hell is promised to all of us who do not live in righteousness." [83] Not only does Pelagius believe in hell for those who do not believe, he also believes hell is reserved for those who fail to choose righteousness, to live in sync with God after they first have faith in Christ through baptism. Pagitt does not go this far, however. Instead he merely suggests that "the afterlife isn't a place. It's a state of being." [84] That state of being is vaguely defined as the state in which God's hope and dreams for the world are fulfilled and come to fruition in the Kingdom right now, with no mention of judgment or a "state of being" for those who do not "faith" in Christ or even partner with God and His dreams. [85] While Pagitt agrees with Pelagius in that humans are called to "[align] their lives with the things of God, with the work of God," he does not go as far as Pelagius to suggest what happens to those who don't, or

---

[82] Rees, "On the Christian Life," 118.

[83] B. R. Rees. "On Divine Law," from *The Letters of Pelagius and His Followers.* (Suffolk, England: The Boydell Press, 1991), 99.

[84] Pagitt, *Christianity,* 222.

[85] Pagitt, *Christianity,* 222.

even those who were aligned and then fall out of alignment.

In summation, while Pelagius and Pagitt agree that the example and pattern of Christ is primary for our "salvation" and "integration with the life of God," they go about it in different ways. Pagitt denies the penal essence of the event of the cross by dismissing the suffering, bloodshed, and death of Christ as reflective of ancient Greek blood god myths. Pelagius on the other hand, acknowledges that Christ's suffering, shed blood, and death actually does something for us. While a more exhaustive study of Pelagius' soteriology is necessary, it appears likely that he believes the cross is penal in essence, recognizing Jesus' suffering and bloodshed provides justification for, salvation from, and forgiveness of sins, while needing the example of Christ to carry us to the end. Pagitt's theology of salvation reduces the cross to mere example. In fact, in so doing he is left only with the example, pattern, way, and teachings of Christ. Th is is likely why Pagitt and the broader Emerging Church focus on following the teachings and example of Jesus: without the penalty of the cross that is all that is left.

Here is where Pagitt agrees with Pelagius: in order to live a life of righteousness, a new example and pattern must replace the old ones found in Adam and others. Th e cross does not save, but the example of Jesus does. While Pelagius believes the cross provides for the forgiveness of past sins through faith and "the holy lather"of baptism, Pelagius does not stop with faith alone, but rather requires disciplined following after the example of Christ to provide for future salvation. Both Pagitt and Pelagius, then, rely upon the example of Christ for ultimate, eschatological salvation, in addition to the inner goodness of humanity to obey and choose integration with God.

CONCLUSION

According to Pagitt's own published work, it is clear he reflects much, if not most, of Pelagius' theology. Pagitt is a Pelagian. From human nature to sin, human will to grace, and salvation to judgment, much of Pagitt's theology mirrors Pelagius'. While Pagitt may want to believe differently, he simply believes *otherly*. Historically, this "other theology" was already addressed by another theologian: Augustine. Though the theological controversy between the two was rancorous and dramatic, Augustine and others already dealt with the "other theology" of Pelagius (and Pagitt) through numerous writings and councils in the 5th century. Back then, what was the response of Augustine to Pelagius and how might Augustine respond to Pagitt if he were alive today? This paper will conclude with Augustine's response to Pelagius' theology of human nature, sin, grace, and salvation.

First, regarding human nature, Augustine acknowledges that at first it was uncorrupt and without sin; at Creation, Adam was faultless. He argues, "But that nature of man in which every one is born from Adam, now wants the Physician, because it is not sound." [86] While Pelagius says all people are born sound, Augustine responds by saying that now, post-Fall, the nature of all

---

[86] Augustine. "On Nature and Grace" from *A Select Library of Nicene and Post-Nicene Fathers*. Volume 5. Edited by Phillip Schaff. (Grand Rapids: Eerdmans Publishing, 1991), 122.

people is corrupted. "Let us not suppose, then, that human nature cannot be corrupted by sin, but rather, believing, from the inspired Scriptures, that it is corrupted by sin."[87] Foundational to Pelagius' theology was the notion that we are good and untainted, and out of that untainted nature we are capable of not sinning. Pelagius "maintained that our human nature actually possesses an inseparable capacity of not at all sinning." [88]   In arguing against this inner capacity, Augustine offers a line from the Lord's Prayer: "Lead us not into temptation, but deliver us from evil." Augustine wonders, "If they already have capacity, why do they pray? Or, what is the evil which they pray to be delivered from?" [89] In other words, why should a person pray to be delivered from evil if he, through his own capacity, can deliver himself and not sin? He goes on to say, "Behold what damage the disobedience of the will has inflicted on man's nature! Let him be permitted to pray that he may be healed! [The nature] is wounded, hurt, damaged, destroyed. It is a true confession of its weakness, not a false defense of its capacity, that it stands in need of. It requires the grace of God." [90]   In response to Pelagius' belief that human nature is not corrupt and is capable on its own not to sin, Augustine replies that human nature must be delivered from evil because it must be healed. That healing comes not from self-will, but from the grace of God.

---

[87] Augustine, "On Nature and Grace," 128.

[88] Augustine, "On Nature and Grace," 141.

[89] Augustine, "On Nature and Grace," 142.

[90] Augustine, "On Nature and Grace," 142.

What disturbed Augustine and others most was Pelagius' view of grace. They objected most that Pelagius did not maintain that it is by the grace of God that a man is able to be without sin. [91] Pelagius and his followers argued that the grace of God actually *is* the nature in which we were created, which enables us to act righteously. [92] According to them, the grace of God is not dispensed through Christ, but through Creation; we are able to sin not because of Christ, but because of our human nature, which is in fact the grace of God. Augustine counters, "This, however, is not the grace which the apostle commends to us through the faith of Jesus Christ. For it is certain that we possess this nature in common with ungodly men and unbelievers; whereas the grace which comes through the faith of Jesus Christ belongs only to them to whom the faith itself appertains." [93] While Pelagius equated grace with the God's creation of a good inner nature, Augustine said the grace of God to which the Scriptures attest comes through faith in Christ. Grace is not from Creation, but from Christ alone.

Augustine was also concerned that Pelagius maintained no other opinion than that the grace of God is given according to our merit. In response, Augustine declares, "God's grace is not given according to our merit...it is given not only where there are no good, but even where there are

---

[91] Augustine, "On Nature and Grace," 139.

[92] Augustine. "On Grace and Free Will" from *A Select Library of Nicene and Post-Nicene Fathers*. Volume 5. Edited by Phillip Schaff. (Grand Rapids: Eerdmans Publishing, 1991), 454.

[93] Augustine, "On Grace and Free Will," 454.

many evil merits preceding."[94]   While Pelagius maintains that humans can choose to do good deeds out of an inner, naturally good capacity—and thus are rewarded by God because of those good deeds—Augustine insists that no man ought to attribute those good deeds to himself, but to God. [95] Furthermore, while Pelagius believes that a man is justified from and forgiven of sins by Christ only at the event of baptism, Augustine believes that the grace of God is with him even into the future to cover not yet committed sins. "It is necessary for a man that he should be not only justified when unrighteous by the grace of God...but that, even after he has become justified by faith, grace should accompany him on his way, and he should lean upon it, let he fall." [96] Augustine's view sharply contrasts with Pelagius who insists that the example of Christ is what "empowers" people to choose the righteous life after baptism. Instead of the grace of God empowering people to choose to live in Christ, people's good inner nature allows them to choose integration with God. Augustine counters, "Man, even when most fully justified, is unable to lead a holy life, if he be not divinely assisted by the eternal light of righteousness." [97]

Finally, Augustine addressed the ultimate results of Pelagius' theology: salvation. Augustine responded by saying Pelagius' view of human nature "causes the grace of Christ to be 'made of none effect,' since it is pretended that

---

[94] Augustine, 'On Grace and Free Will," 449.

[95] Augustine, 'On Grace and Free Will," 449.

[96] Augustine, 'On Grace and Free Will," 449.

[97] Augustine, 'On Nature and Grace," 129.

human nature is sufficient for its own holiness and justification." [98]   In reality, neither the cross of Christ nor the grace of God is necessary if humans, through their own inner nature, can pull themselves up by their own bootstraps. Augustine counters Pelagius' faith in human nature by saying, "if the righteousness came from nature, then Christ is dead in vain." [99]   If the grace of God came through nature and out of our own inner capacity we can attain to right living, rather than through faith in Christ, then Christ's death was in vain. Augustine maintained that the same faith which restored the saints of old now restores us: "that is to say, faith 'in the one Mediator between God and men, the man Christ Jesus,'—faith in His blood, faith in His cross, faith in His death and resurrection." [100] While Pelagius believes a person is justified, saved, and forgiven when a person comes in faith to Christ through baptism, he does not believe that faith alone is sufficient for salvation. Instead, faith and deeds ultimately bring and secure eternal life into the future. Augustine wishes Pelagius would meditate on Acts 4:12, which says, "There is no other name under heaven given by which we must be saved," "and that [Pelagius] would not so uphold the possibility of human nature, as to believe that man can be saved by free will without the Name!" [101]

In many ways, the same conclusions arrived at by Augustine of Pelagius could be applied to Pagitt. Because

---

[98] Augustine, "On Nature and Grace," 141.

[99] Augustine, "On Grace and Free Will," 454.

[100] Augustine, "On Nature and Grace," 139.

[101] Augustine, "On Nature and Grace," 137.

Pagitt clearly mirrors a substantial amount of Pelagius' theology on humanity, sin, and salvation, one could imagine similar criticism from Augustine of Pagitt. Augustine might tell Pagitt that we do not have the light of God within us still, but rather are broken and tainted because of sin. In response to Pagitt's newborn analogy, Augustine would maintain that we are born sinners and are in need of healing from birth. Furthermore, Augustine might insist that the systems, hurts, and patterns of this world are not to blame for living lives of disintegration, rather we sin because we are naturally sinful; examples, habits, and ignorance does not lead us into sin, our nature does. Salvifically, Augustine would probably declare that the event of the cross, with all of its suffering, bloodshed, and death, is of the utmost importance because of the real, tangible expression and dispensation of grace it bore for the world. We need Christ, not simply for His example and pattern, but for the grace and salvation He brings us through the event of the cross. Christ is not simply our map, guide, and new example, He is our Savior and Redeemer. Augustine would maintain that we can live integrated lives with God by obeying Him, rather than living out of our sinful nature, because of the grace He gives us through faith in Jesus Christ alone, not because Jesus' example is better than the rest.

As quoted from Olson in the beginning, the story of Christian theology is about the historical reflection on the nature of salvation. Likewise, an examination of Pagitt, Pelagius, and Augustine is not simply an exercise in parsing theological positions on the nature of humanity and original sin, it's about the gospel of Jesus Christ. According to this examination, Pagitt's Christianity is not a different, more hopeful faith, it is an other form of faith that both the Communion of Saints and Spirit of God have deemed foreign to the Holy Scriptures, Rule of Faith, and gospel of Jesus Christ. One question remains, however: How will the contemporary American Communion deem this other faith?

BIBLIOGRAPHY

Augustine. "On Nature and Grace" from A Select Library of Nicene and Post-Nicene Fathers. Volume 5. Edited by Phillip Schaff. Grand Rapids: Eerdmans Publishing, 1991.

_____. "On Grace and Free Will" from A Select Library of Nicene and Post-Nicene Fathers. Volume 5. Edited by Phillip Schaff. Grand Rapids: Eerdmans Publishing, 1991.

Frend, W. C. H. Th e Rise of Christianity. Philadelphia: Fortress Press, 1984.

Jones, Tony. Th e New Christians. San Francisco: Jossey-Bass, 2007.

_____ "Original Sin: A Depraved Idea." 26 January 2009. http://blog.beliefnet.com/tonyjones/2009/01/original-sin-a-depraved-idea.html.

_____ "Original Sin: Th e Genesis of a Doctrine." 29 January 2009. http://blog.beliefnet.com/tonyjones/ 2009/01/original-sin-the-genesis-of-a.html.

_____ "Original Sin: Paul, Romans 5, and the Heart of the Issue." 16 February 2009. http://blog.beliefnet.com/ tonyjones/2009/02/original-sin-paul-romans-5- and.html.

McLaren, Brian. Th e Story We Find Ourselves In. San Francisco: Jossey-Bass, 2003.

Olson, Roger E. The Story of Christian Theology. Downers Grove, IL: IVP Academic, 1999.

Pagitt, Doug. A Christianity Worth Believing. San Francisco: Jossey-Bass, 2007.

Pelagius. "To Demetrias." Pages 29-70 in Th e Letters of Pelagius and His Followers. Translated by B. R. Rees. Suffolk, England: The Boydell Press, 1991.

_____. "On Divine Law." Pages 88-104 in The Letters of Pelagius and His Followers. Translated by B. R. Rees. Suffolk, England: The Boydell Press, 1991.

_____. "On the Christian Life." Pages 105-126. The Letters of Pelagius and His Followers. Translated by B. R. Rees. Suffolk, England: The Boydell Press, 1991.

_____. "To an Old Friend." Pages 147-154 in The Letters of Pelagius and His Followers. Translated by B. R. Rees. Suffolk, England: The Boydell Press, 1991.

_____. "On Bad Teachers." Pages 214-235 in The Letters of Pelagius and His Followers. Translated by B. R. Rees. Suffolk, England: The Boydell Press, 1991.

_____. Pelagius' Commentary on St. Paul's Epistle to the Romans. Translated by Theodore De Bruyn. Oxford: Clarendon Paperbacks, 1998.

Reimagining the Christian Faith

Essay 2
Rollins, Selmanovic, & Barth

In 2007, Doug Pagitt and Tony Jones co-edited a book called *An Emergent Manifesto of Hope*. At the time, Tony Jones was the National Coordinator of Emergent Village, a national coordinating organization for the progressive Evangelical "conversation" known as the emerging church. Likewise, Doug Pagitt was one of the founding members of Emergent and editor of the newly-minted Emersion line of books from Baker Publishing Group out of which this title was published. The book was a collection of "voices" within the broader conversation "attempting to sing a song together" (whether or not the harmonies matched) in order to provide context for and explain what exactly was being sung within the Emergent Church. [1] One such voice was Chris Erdman who wrote a piece on the venerable Swiss theologian Karl Barth.

In the Emergent Church conversation Barth is considered a so-called "Friend of Emergent" who supposedly supports the key questions and answers percolating within the Emerging conversation. In his article, "Digging Up the Past: Karl Barth (the Reformed Giant) as Friend to the Emerging Church," Erdman attempts to establish that Barth is Emergent's friend and theological ally. Erdman likes Barth because he insisted that "the theological enterprise must never be the sole realm of academic theologians" and because he believed "the theological imperative was never finished." [2] Similarly, leaders in the Emergent Church call on the Church as it currently exists to wrench theological work from the hands of the elite and put it firmly into the hands of the people, in order to ensure theological inquiry and development is "never static, never dull, never fixed, always open." [3]   As Erdman insists, "We now, like Barth then, are dissatisfied with the established and entrenched theology that has produced our present crisis. We seek another way; we want to 'begin all over again,' to work in a state of 'constant

---

[1] Tony Jones, "Introduction: Friendship, Faith, and Going Somewhere Together" in *An Emergent Manifesto of Hope* (ed. by Doug Pagitt and Tony Jones; Grand Rapids: Baker Books, 2007), 14.

[2] Chris Erdman, "Digging Up the Past: Karl Barth (the Reformed Giant) as Friend to the Emerging Church" in *An Emergent Manifesto of Hope* (ed. Doug Pagitt and Tony Jones; Grand Rapids: Baker Books, 2007), 238.

[3] Erdman, "Digging Up the Past," 239.

emergency.'"[4] Th e only problem is that the theological work and "other way" born out of that dissatisfaction would be questioned and confronted by Barth himself, rather than supported.

Though the Emergent Church may find companionship in Barth's own theological journey, he is much more a foe than friend to what that journey has produced. Upon surveying the theological fruit birthed from two influential emerging church thinkers—Peter Rollins and Samir Selmanovic[5] —and digging into the particulars of Barth's own theology,[6] this essay will reveal how Barth is an adversary to the emerging church in a particularly important area of theological discourse, the doctrine of revelation. Rollins understands the revelation of God in two key ways: 1) the hiddenness and hyper-

---

[4] Erdman, "Digging Up the Past," 240.

[5] Hailing from Belfast, Ireland, Peter Rollins is an up-and-comer within the Emergent Church conversation who has written on our (in)ability to speak of God by exploring the doctrine of the revelation of God. His book, *How (not) to Speak of God* (Brewster, MA: Paraclete Press, 2006.) is described as offering "an unprecedented message of transformation that has the potential to revolutionize the theological architecture of Western Christianity."

Samir Selmanovic is a founder and Christian co-leader of Faith House Manhattan, an interfaith community that brings together "forward-looking Christian, Muslims, Jews, atheists, and others who seek to thrive interdependently." He has also served on the Coordinating Group for Emergent Village, is the director of a Christian community in New York City called *Citylights*, and serves on the Interfaith Relations commission of the National Council of Churches.

[6] Karl Barth, *Church Dogmatics*, vol. I,1: *The Doctrine of the Word of God* (trans. G.T. Thomson. Edinburgh: T.&T. Clark, 1936); Karl Barth, *Church Dogmatics*, vol. II,1: *The Doctrine of God* (ed. G.W. Bromiley and T.F. Torrance; trans. T.H.L Parker, W.B. Johnson, Harold Knight, and J.L.M. Haire. Edinburgh: T.&T. Clark, 1957).

transcendence of God, resulting in a thickly veiled God who isn't truly knowable; and 2) our inability to say anything directly of God Himself, resulting in speech that never speaks of God but merely our understanding of God. While Selmanovic does believes God is revealed and known to humanity, that revelation and knowledge is neither contained within the "Christian religion" nor exclusively in Jesus Christ. Consequently, God is trans-religious and is also revealed beyond the person of Jesus Christ. Barth will counter both theologians by insisting the revelation of God is "clear and certain" and is exclusively in Jesus Christ.

While Barth insists that theology is "nothing but human 'language about God'" [7] he still insists there is something to say. In fact, a whole lot to say. And because the theological discipline of dogmatics is the servant of Church proclamation, [8] that "something" should be proclaimed well and in accordance with the Holy Scriptures, for the glory of God and good of the world. In the end, Barth will reveal how what Rollins and Selmanovic are saying is neither in one accord with the Scriptures nor part of the historic Christian faith.

GOD CAN BE KNOWN

In *How (Not) to Speak of God*, Rollins operates from the assumption that, "That which we cannot speak of is the one thing about whom and to whom we must never stop

---

[7] Barth, *Church Dogmatics*, vol. I,1:3.

[8] Barth, *Church Dogmatics*, vol. I,1:92.

speaking." [9] Though we are called to continually speak of God, we cannot actually speak of or describe Him. Throughout this rhetorical tour de force, Rollins' book attempts to re-understand the traditional understanding of the nature of God's self-disclosure. As Rollins explains, traditionally Christianity has rested upon the idea that God has communicated to humanity through revelation, a concept that has been known as "that which reveals," is the opposite of concealment, and God has graciously disclosed to us something about himself. [10] In other words, in the past the historic doctrine of revelation that meant God has actually revealed, de-concealed, and graciously disclosed Himself to the world. In fact, Rollins suggests it is thought that "Christianity...has privileged access to the mind of God," an access which is contained and controlled by Christianity alone. [11] Rollins believes otherwise.

According to Rollins, this idea of revelation came through the Enlightenment after Christianity (falsely) embraced the Age of Reason, believing that "God was open to our understanding insomuch as God was revealed to us through the scripture." [12]   For these Enlightenment Christians, it was simple: God gave us a document (the Holy Scriptures) and the ability to understand and explore that document (the mind), thus providing access to God's full, real Self (revelation). For Rollins, however, this notion

[9] Pete Rollins, *How (Not) to Speak of God* (Brewster, MA: Paraclete Press, 2006, xii.

[10] Rollins, *How (Not) to Speak of God*, 7.

[11] Rollins, *How (Not) to Speak of God*, 7.

[12] Rollins, *How (Not) to Speak of God*, 9.

of theistic accessibility is nothing short of "conceptual idolatry." He insists the idea of any system of thought which the individual or community takes to be a visible rendering of God—in this case an intellectual rendering—is neither God nor of God, but is instead an anthropocentric construct, an idol. [13] Rollins insists that Western theology has reduced God to conceptual idols by the very exercise of naming God. Instead, Rollins suggests God is not only unnameable, He is "omninameable," he cannot be revealed through human words and at the site of revelation, even when we think we can see God revealed to us, "we can only speak of God's otherness and distance; Revelation has concealment built into its very heart." [14]

Rollins believes that Christianity has far too much confidence in a full divine self-disclosure, too much confidence in an actual complete revelation at God's own behest, resulting in an overly defined, imbued "God" term. As Rollins insists, "If we fail to recognize that the term 'God' always falls short of that towards which the word is supposed to point, we will end up bowing down before our own conceptual creations forged from the raw materials of our self-image, rather than bowing before the one who stands over and above that creation." [15]   According to Rollins, Christianity—especially the Western variety—has and is bowing before self-made revelatory "blocks of wood" in the form of theological constructs. He believes these constructs never really point to God Himself, however,

---

[13] Rollins, *How (Not) to Speak of God*, 12.

[14] Rollins, *How (Not) to Speak of God*, 12.

[15] Rollins, *Speak of God*, 19.

because God blinds us with too much information about Himself. We must realize that our understanding of God comes as a result of One who overflows and blinds our understanding; God's incoming blinds our intellect, saturates our understanding with a blinding presence, and gives us far too much information, resulting in an intellectual "short-circuiting" by the excess of presence. [16] Ironically, while he argues God blinds us with the light of His presence, Rollins also agrees with Gregory of Nyssa that the more we move toward God we journey into divine darkness. While religious knowledge begins as an experience of entering into the light, the deeper we go the more darkness we find in that light; God is beyond the reach of all thinking. [17] In short, "Christianity testifies to the impossibility of grasping God because of the hyper-presence of God." [18] Barth would suggest otherwise, however.

For Barth, humanity has actual, genuine knowledge of God because God has chosen to actually, genuinely disclose Himself to us. Through His own purpose and volition, God made the decision to encounter man. As Barth argues, "God encounters man in such a way that man can know Him. He encounters him in such a way that in this encounter He still remains God, but also raises man up to be a real, genuine knower of Himself." [19] Rather than being hyper-hidden and overly concealed, God sets Himself

---

[16] Rollins, *Speak of God*, 22, 24.

[17] Rollins, *Speak of God*, 27.

[18] Rollins, *Speak of God*, 46.

[19] Barth, *Church Dogmatics*, II,1:32.

before man in such away that he can actually and genuinely speak of and describe God. In other words, God is "graspable" by the very fact He has placed Himself before man to be grasped. In fact, though Barth does acknowledge a hiddenness and mystery to even His revelation, he also insists that God has made Himself "clear and certain to us;" God does not remain hidden to us, but we have a knowledge from God Himself. [20]   We can actually, genuinely know God because He has chosen to show Himself to us in such a way that we can consider and conceive Him. [21]   What we must understand, however, is that this knowledge is not from us, but from God.

This knowledge of which we speak "cannot at any moment or in any respect try to understand itself other than as the knowledge made possible, realized and ordered by God alone." [22]   Like Barth, this is somewhat the point Rollins attempts to make: the source of our desire (God) is set as an object that we reflect upon in order to grasp it, hold it. [23]   In an effort to maintain God's "otherness" and "beyondness," however, Rollins ultimately makes God unreachable and unknowable. Furthermore, Rollins argues that even when we describe God and claim a knowledge of Him, that claim and knowledge isn't even God Himself, but merely our *understanding* of God. [24]   Barth would strongly

---

[20] Barth, *Church Dogmatics*, II,1:39.

[21] Barth, *Church Dogmatics*, II,1:10.

[22] Barth, *Church Dogmatics*, II,1:41.

[23] Rollins, *Speak of God*, 1-2.

[24] Rollins, *Speak of God*, 98.

insist otherwise, however. In fact he did: "there is a readiness of God to be known as *He actually is known* in the fulfillment in which the knowledge of God is a fact." [25] Rather than being hyper-hidden and our God-talk other than God Himself, God can be known because God wants to be known and what we say of God, by His grace, actually speaks of God. Barth continues: "'God is knowable' means God can be known—He can be known of and by Himself; in His essence, as it is turned to us in His activity, He is so constituted that He can be known by us." [26] In sharp contrast to Rollins, Barth rightly asserts that God has in fact set Himself before man in such away that we can confidently say "God can be known."

While human efforts at accurately and exhaustively describing God are fraught with inconsistencies, fragility, and incompleteness because man is fallen and sinful, we can know God because He has revealed Himself to humanity to be known. As Barth explains, "God makes Himself known and offers Himself to us, so that we can in fact love Him as the one who exists for us...and He creates in us the possibility—the willingness and readiness—to know Him; so that, seen from our side also, there is no reason why this should not actually happen." [27] Actual, genuine knowledge of God can "actually happen" because we have a revelation from Him that comes to us in a manner that is intelligible, accessible, and clear. This revelation is clear, accessible, and intelligible not because

---

[25] Barth, *Church Dogmatics*, II,1:65. (emph. mine)

[26] Barth, *Church Dogmatics*, II,1:65.

[27] Barth, *Church Dogmatics*, II,1:33.

we ourselves are capable of thinking our way to God through our own gumption and ingenuity, though. Barth makes it clear that, "it is by the grace of God and only by the grace of God that it comes about that God is knowable to us...He gives Himself to us to be known, which establishes our knowledge of Him. God's revelation is not at our power and command, but happens as a movement 'from God.'" [28] Barth also makes it incredibly clear that this ultimate movement of God to reveal Himself to humanity was through Jesus Christ, an assertion that is as questioned as our ability to even know God.

GOD'S REVELATION IS JESUS CHRIST

Not only does the Emergent Church question our ability to know God and challenge the extent to which God has truly spoken, the center of that knowledge and speaking is questioned, too. From the beginning, the historic Christian faith has taken seriously Jesus' own claim in John 14:9 that, "Anyone who has seen me has seen the Father." In the past, it was believed that God the Father was revealed in God the Son, the One True God is only found in Jesus Christ. Now, however, even this central claim of historic Christian orthodoxy is questioned. In an essay in An Emergent Manifesto of Hope, Samir Selmanovic spearheaded this questioning when he claims, "We do believe that God is best defined by the historical revelation in Jesus Christ, but to believe that God is limited to it would be an attempt to manage God. If one holds that Christ is confined to Christianity, one has chosen a god

---

[28] Barth, *Church Dogmatics*, II,1:69.

that is not sovereign." [29]   He writes elsewhere that the revelation of the grace of God through Jesus Christ, which has always been central to the historic Christian faith, is not exclusively limited to that faith or Jesus Christ. As Selmanovic claims, "We Christians have insisted that our revelation is the only container and only dispenser of grace. The rest of the world, graced from within, has been steadily proving us wrong. Grace is independent." [30]   Selmanovic baldly asserts that the revelation that has come through the Holy Scriptures and Jesus Christ himself are not the only containers of God's grace; grace is also found outside the Christian Story. According to Selmanovic, neither the revelation of God Himself nor of His grace is contained or confined to Jesus Christ.

In *It's Really All About God: Reflections of a Muslim Atheist Jewish Christian,* Selmanovic revises and extends these initial thoughts on God's Christian containment. He argues, "to say God has decided to visit all humanity through only one particular religion is a deeply unsatisfying assertion about God." [31]   In order to protect his argument in favor of religious pluralism, Selmanovic claims that none of us are in charge of God; God refuses to be owned and to comply with our religious constructs. [32] In

---

[29] Samir Selmanovic, "The Sweet Problem of Inclusivism," (ed. Doug Pagitt and Tony Jones; Grand Rapids: BakerBooks, 2007), 193. (emph. mine)

[30] Samir Selmanovic, *It's Really All About God: Reflections of a Muslim Atheist Jewish Christian* (San Francisco: Jossey-Bass, 2009), 52.

[31] Selmanovic, *All About God*, 9.

[32] Selmanovic, *About God*, 16, 18.

fact Selmanovic argues strongly for a revelation beyond that of the Christian faith:

> As long as those of us who are Christians insist on staying enclosed in our own world of meanings, we have nothing more to say to the world. Without recognizing God, grace, and goodness outside of the boundaries we have made and without the possibility of expanding our understanding of God, grace, and goodness, we have come to a place where Christianity as we know it must either end or experience another Exodus. [33]

Here Selmanovic insists that Christians must acknowledge that God is everywhere—in every person, every community, and all creation—otherwise we will loose the basis for seeing God anywhere.[34] Ultimately, Selmanovic believes that "the Christianity that claims exclusive possession of God's revelation in the person of Jesus has hijacked that same God from the world." [35] After reducing Christianity to one of three monotheistic "religions," Selmanovic shows his real hand: "People want God, but not one who is the captive of a religion. Th ey want an unmanaged God. Free God. Th at's where hope comes from." [36] Apparently, Selmanovic also desires a God free from religion, Christianity, Jesus Christ.

---

[33] Selmanovic, *About God*, 60-61.

[34] Selmanovic, *About God*, 60-61.

[35] Selmanovic, *About God*, 68.

[36] Selmanovic, *About God*, 90, 92.

Barth paints a very different picture in his *Dogmatics*, however. He boldly asserts that God's revelation is only, exclusively in Jesus Christ. While Selmanovic believes that God is simply best defined by the historical revelation in Jesus Christ, Barth insists God is *only* defined by Jesus Christ. To suggest that God is not limited to "the historical revelation in Jesus Christ" is foreign to the Holy Scriptures and historic Christian faith. Barth argues this very point when he writes, "[God] is wholly and utterly in His revelation in Jesus Christ." [37] He also makes plain that we must know Jesus in order to know God, because "in him are hid all the treasures of wisdom and knowledge (Col. 2:3)." [38] Furthermore, Barth makes clear that what he describes in his *Dogmatics* is the knowledge of God as found in the knowledge of Jesus; unless Jesus Christ is the reference point for the revelation of God, "we have not described it in faith, or as the knowledge of faith, and therefore not in any sense as the true knowledge of God." [39]

While Selmanovic believes that "Grace did not start with Christianity and will not end with Christianity. It is a common thing in this world." [40] Barth argues otherwise: "When we appeal to God's grace, we appeal to the grace of the incarnation and to [Jesus Christ] as the One in whom, because He is the eternal Son of God, knowledge of God

---

[37] Barth, *Church Dogmatics*, II,1:75.

[38] Barth, *Church Dogmatics*, II,1:252.

[39] Barth, *Church Dogmatics*, II,1:252.

[40] Selmanovic, *About God*, 51.

was, is and will be present originally and properly." [41] For Barth, the revelation of God through grace is intimately and only connected to Jesus Christ, because His own act of divine self-disclosure is bound up with Him. Jesus Christ is given to the whole being of God, not simply a part of Him, and God is not known at all unless He is known in His entirety as Father, Son and Holy Spirit, Creator, Reconciler, and Redeemer. [42] It is in His grace through Jesus Christ that God is known as Reconciler and Redeemer. Rather than experiencing the knowledge of God and His grace apart from Jesus Christ, both are intimately and only connected to *Him*. It is only in Jesus Christ that we know and understand God and His grace.

Selmanovic goes on to rhetorically wonder, however, "Is our religion the only one that understands the true meaning of life? Or does God place his truth in others too? Well, God decides, and not us. The gospel is not our gospel, but the gospel of the kingdom of God, and what belongs to the kingdom of God cannot be hijacked by Christianity." [43] In this argument Selmanovic does two things: 1) he argues that the Kingdom of God is not connect simply to Jesus; and 2) he argues the Kingdom of God itself is a vehicle of what Barth call's "divine immanence." Barth, however, makes it clear that God's Kingdom is not known at all apart from Jesus Christ, and attempting to do so is heretical. As Barth strongly warns, "Christian heresies spring from the fact that man does not take seriously the known ground of

---

[41] Barth, *Church Dogmatics*, II,1:252.

[42] Barth, *Church Dogmatics*, II,1:51-52.

[43] Selmanovic, "The Sweet Problem of Inclusivism," 194.

divine immanence in Jesus Christ, so that from its revelation, instead of apprehending Jesus Christ and the totality in Him, he arbitrarily selects this or that feature and sets it up as a subordinate centre: perhaps the idea of creation...or even the kingdom of God." [44] It seems clear that Selmanovic is in danger of making the very mistake Barth warns against for two reasons.

First, Selmanovic clearly describes the Kingdom of God in terms that are utterly disconnected from Jesus Christ alone. Secondly, he has selected the feature of the Kingdom of God and believes it as a revelatory ground of "divine immanence," instead of Jesus Christ alone. Barth counters such people with these words:

> oblivious of the fact that [divine] immanence both as a whole and in its parts has Christian truth and reality only in so far as it is founded in Jesus Christ and summed up in Him, so that if, as a whole and in its parts, it is affirmed, preached and believed as a centre in itself and alongside Christ, the Church will inevitably be led back into heathendom and its worship of the elements. [45]

Unfortunately, Selmanovic affirms this devastating indictment by claiming the Kingdom is not exclusively limited to Jesus Christ. I quote him at length:

> Many Christians believe that the Kingdom of God that Jesus spoke about is inseparable from

---

[44] Barth, *Church Dogmatics*, II,1:319.

[45] Barth, *Church Dogmatics*, II,1:319.

> knowing the person of Jesus. If so, the question begs to be asked: Is the Kingdom of God present in all of life, among all people, throughout history, or is the Kingdom of God limited to the historical person of Jesus and thus absent from most of life, most people, and most history? The answer to this question depends greatly on whether Christians are willing to make their religion take a backseat to something larger than itself. [46]

It seems clear that Selmanovic completely disconnects God's revelation from the person of Jesus Christ, while making it no longer exclusively connected to him. In light of these observations it seems clear enough from Selmanovic's arguments that the Kingdom of God, as part of divine immanence, has been wrested from its moorings in Jesus Christ and is "affirmed, preached and believed as a centre in itself and *alongside* Christ." God is now revealed in the Kingdom of God and alongside Jesus Christ, rather than through Him alone.

Not only does he believe that the Kingdom of God apart from Jesus Christ reveals God, Selmanovic denies that God is revealed fully and exclusively in Christ. Selmanovic both favors another revelation of God apart from Jesus Christ (the Kingdom of God) and denies that the fulness of God's revelation is in Him alone. As Barth reminds us, though, "Any deviation, any attempt to evade Jesus Christ in favor of another supposed revelation of God, or any denial of the fulness of God's presence in Him, will precipitate us into darkness and confusion." According

---

[46] Selmanovic, *All About God*, 76-77.

to Barth, then, Selmanovic's belief that God is revealed in a separate act of divine immanence (the Kingdom of God) apart from Jesus Christ "will precipitate us into darkness and confusion." [47] Likewise, Selmanovic assertion that God is not revealed wholly, simply, exclusively in Jesus Christ will have the same result. It is clear that Selmanovic's belief in the revelation and knowledge of God largely departs from the historic Christian faith. In response Barth would adamantly declare it is really not all about God. It is really all about Jesus Christ.

CONCLUSION

Thanks to these Emergent leaders, there is now growing confusion within the Church over both the extent to which we may know God and the manner in which He has revealed Himself. It seems clear that Rollins understands God as hyper-transcendent and Wholly Other, believing He is far more hidden and concealed than the Christian faith believes. For Rollins we can neither truly name God nor actually describe Him, because He is not actually, genuinely revealed. Practically, this cashes out as what Rollins calls an "a/theistic Christianity." An a/theistic Christian can be said to operate with a discourse that makes claims about God while simultaneously acknowledging that these claims are provisional, uncertain, and insufficient; our questioning of God isn't really questioning of God Himself but only a means of questioning our *understanding* of God. [48] By implication

---

[47] Barth, *Church Dogmatics*, II,1:319.

[48] Rollins, *Speak of God*, 98.

this would mean the revelation we have of God is not complete or actual enough to understand, question, and know Him. Th is is why Rollins ultimately insists that speaking of God is really only speaking about our understanding of God, rather than God himself. [49]

Selmanovic, while acknowledging a real revelation of God that can be experienced by humans, believes that revelation is neither exclusively tied to Jesus Christ nor contained within the Christian faith. For Him, it's really all about "God," a vapid, generalized World-Spirit [50] that is encased in all religions, rather than exclusively revealed through Jesus Christ, on the one hand, and the Church, on the other. Selmanovic is unsatisfied with the assertion that the Christian faith testifies to God's Story of Rescue and that rescue is exclusively found in Jesus Christ. In fact, the grace of God to which the Holy Scriptures and Church have testified for generations isn't even unique to the Christ or the Christian faith. Instead, this grace is independent from both and common in the world's histories, stories, and religions. God is present everywhere and in every person, and the Christian faith cannot insist on an exclusive revelation in Jesus Christ or the Church. In the end, it is the Kingdom of God that reveals God to the world, an idea that is trans-religious and separate from even Jesus Christ Himself.

Upon surveying the writings of both Rollins and Selmanovic, one wonders why they are self-described Christians and committed to Christianity at all. If God

---

[49] Rollins, *Speak of God*, 32.

[50] This is the same language Fredrick Schleiermacher uses in his book, *On Religion*.

doesn't really speak, why posture one's self as a listener? If God is not wholly and exclusively revealed in Jesus Christ, why commit one's self to Him and His Story? In response to both religious thinkers, Barth asserts God does speak and He is revealed in Jesus Christ. For Barth, there is real, genuine knowledge of God because God has chosen to reveal Himself to humanity. This divine self-disclosure is in such away that humans can actually, genuinely know Him. Barth declares that there is a readiness of God to be known, a knowledge that is "clear and certain." While the knowledge that we have is not through our own gumption and ingenuity, but through grace, God is revealed in such a way that we can know Him. Though we cannot apprehend this revelation through our own power and will, it does happen and has happened. Barth makes clear that ultimately Jesus Christ is the point at which the world truly knows God. While others may suggest God is *best* defined by Jesus Christ, Barth insists He is *only* defined by Jesus. God is utterly and wholly revealed in Jesus Christ; to know Jesus is to know God. In fact, the only way to know God in intimate relationship is through the grace found in and through Jesus Christ. Barth maintains that God's grace is only and intimately connected to Christ, rather than other sources and other religious faiths. Finally, Barth warns of the danger of selecting competing centers of revelation apart from Jesus Christ, like the Kingdom of God.

In his *Church Dogmatics* volume on *The Doctrine of God*, Barth makes clear that "Theology guides the language of the Church, so far as it concretely reminds her that in all circumstances it is fallible human work, which in the matter of relevance or irrelevance lies in the balance, and must obedience to grace, if it is to be well done." [51]   Here Barth acknowledges the difficult task of "theologizing," of speaking of God and His acts. While that speech is fallible and vacillates between relevance or irrelevance, requiring a healthy dose of grace along the way, it needs to happen nonetheless. Every generation needs to cherish, protect, and contend for the Rule of Faith given by our Lord once to the Church. If not, there is a real danger of precipitating into darkness and confusion. It is clear from the writings of these two theologians and thinkers that a shift is occurring within the Church regarding an important piece of that Rule, revelation.

Though historic Christian orthodoxy has consistently held to the real, genuine knowability of God and that knowledge being fully and exclusively revealed (outside of creation) in Jesus Christ, there are some who insist otherwise. Th ere is a growing number who shove God so far into the clouds that nothing can be concretely said of Him. Others still, and perhaps more dangerously so, fi nd God outside Jesus Christ, insisting God is in every person, every community, every religion. God and His grace is no longer exclusively revealed in Jesus Christ, but possessed by other faiths, too. It is worth ending with Barth's warning as a reminder for these   theologians and other Christians: "Any deviation, any attempt to evade Jesus Christ in favor of another supposed revelation of God, or any denial of the fulness of God's presence in Him, will precipitate us into darkness and confusion." [52]

---

[51] Karl Barth, *Church Dogmatics*, vol. I,1:2.

[52] Karl Barth, *Church Dogmatics*, vol. I,1:2.

May this not be the end of these or others who claim Jesus Christ as Lord.

BIBLIOGRAPHY

Barth, Karl. Church Dogmatics, vol I, 1: Th e Doctrine of the Word of God. Translated by G.T. Th omson. Edinburgh: T&T Clark, 1955.

_____. Church Dogmatics, vol II, 1: Th e Doctrine of God. Edited by G.W. Bromiley and T.F. Torrance. Translated by T.H.L Parker, W.B. Johnson, Harold Knight, and J.L.M. Haire. Edinburgh: T&T Clark, 1957.

Erdman, Chris. "Digging Up the Past: Karl Barth (the Reformed Giant) as Friend to the Emerging Church," Pages 236-243 in An Emergent Manifesto of Hope. Edited by Doug Pagitt and Tony Jones. Grand Rapids: Baker Books, 2007.

Jones, Tony. "Introduction: Friendship, Faith, and Going Somewhere Together." Pages 11-15 in An Emergent Manifesto of Hope. Edited by Doug Pagitt and Tony Jones. Grand Rapids: Baker Books, 2007.

Rollins, Pete. How (Not) To Speak of God. Brewster, MA: Paraclete Press, 2006.

Selmanovic, Samir. "The Sweet Problem of Inclusivism." Pages 11-15 in An Emergent Manifesto of Hope. Edited by Doug Pagitt and Tony Jones. Grand Rapids: Baker Books, 2007.

_____. It's Really All About God: Reflections of a Muslim Atheist Jewish Christian. San Francisco: Jossey-Bass, 2009.

Essay 3
McLaren & Ritschl

In 2001 Brian McLaren, a little known pastor author just north of Washington D.C.,[1] began influencing street-level theological conversations within evangelicalism with his landmark book, *A New Kind of Christian*. Through the book's two protagonists—Pastor Dan and Neo— McLaren took the reader on a redefining journey through evangelical's core theological doctrines. God, creation, sin, Christ, the cross, resurrection, and judgment were all addressed and countered with alternative possibilities that formed the foundation for a broader conversation known as the Emerging Church. It was also a reflection of his own

---

[1] McLaren has since retired from pastoring and been named one of the "25 Most Influential Evangelicals In America," *Time Magazine*, February 7, 2005.

spiritual journey, one that culminated in "a quest for honesty, for authenticity, and for a faith that made more sense to me and to others...learning that there is a kind of faith that runs deeper than mere beliefs."[2] Many who entered this conversation found resonance with McLaren's quest, fi nding solace in the questions and alternative answers offered by McLaren in response to what many perceived to be stogy, stuffy, stale theology that had outlived its lifecycle. While the *New Kind of Christian* trilogy simply offered possibilities, McLaren's latest book, *A New Kind of Christianity*, suggests concrete alternatives to the historic Christian faith.

A New Kind of Christianity, the culmination of McLaren's work, is a theological tour de force that continues the Emerging Church's theological challenge, while offering theological alternatives in the process. Now rather than simply translating the historic Christian faith into a present postmodern context, McLaren insists "we need a new way of believing, not simply new answers to the same old questions, but a new set of questions. We are acknowledging that the Christianities we have created deserve to be reexamined and deconstructed...so that our religious traditions can be seen for what they are...they are evolving, embodied, situated versions of the faith."[3] Like others, McLaren has set out to construct a new, fresh, alternative Christianity.

There isn't anything new, however, about the main tenets of this newly constructed version of Christianity.

---

2 Brian McLaren, *A New Kind of Christianity* (New York, HarperOne, 2010,) 6, 8.

3 McLaren, *New Kind of Christianity*, 18, 27.

Instead, the version of Christianity offered by the Emerging Church and its leaders is a repackaged form of other versions that have appeared throughout the historical progression of the story of Christian theology. McLaren's newest theological missive to the church is no different. Though he believes a new kind of Christianity "is trying to be born among those of us who believe and follow Jesus Christ,"[4] McLaren's version of Christianity is an old one; specifically A New Kind of Christianity is a repackaged form of the Christian faith known as Ritschlianism, the theology of Albrect Ritschl, a German theologian who followed in the theological footsteps of Fredrick Schleiermacher, the father of modern-day liberalism. [5]

Shortly after his death, Ritschl was said to have done "more than any other theologian to prepare the way for a fundamental and yet conservative reconstruction of the theology of the church." [6]   Th ough perhaps not as well known as his predecessor, Schleiermacher, Ritschl has been a significant theological force within liberal Protestantism, having influenced a generation of Western theologians and theological movements through his theological reconstruction. He had a profound impact on Adolf von Harnack,[7] who is credited with inaugurating the century-long Historic Jesus Movement. Walter Rauschenbush, a

---

[4] McLaren, *New Kind of Christianity*, 13.

[5] Olson, *The Story of Christian Theology* (Downers Grove: IVP Academic, 1999), 542.

[6] Albert Temple Swing, The Theology of Albrect Ritschl (London: Longmans, Green, and Co., 1901), 1.

[7] Livingston, James C. *Modern Christian Thought*, (New York: Macmillian Publishing Co., 1971.), 257, 258.

Baptist preacher from upstate New York, drew upon the theological themes of Ritschl while founding the so-called Social Justice Movement. [8]   One also finds elements of Ritschl in Paul Tillich, one of the four most influential theologians of the 20th century who helped give rise to Christian existentialism. [9]   Following in the theological tradition of these 19th and 20th century theologians is a 21st century voice, Brian McLaren.

Because of the nature and influence of the contemporary emerging church movement in general and McLaren in particular, it is necessary to engage his writings. Currently, very few are placing the writings of these leaders under the lens of historical theology; very few historical theologian gave engaged McLaren's newest theological work. Therefore, this examination will explore McLaren's writings, with special emphasis on A New Kind of Christianity, in light of the theology of Ritschl. This theological comparison will map the theological similarities between Ritschl and McLaren in three key theological categories: sin, Christology, and salvation.

First, we will explore how they view humanity's problem through their view on sin. Second, we will look at why they say Christ was necessary and how our sin problem is solved through His work. Finally, we will seek to understand how we find salvation and from what we are saved in the first place. In the end, this comparative analysis will reveal McLaren's Christianity is not new at all. It is a repackaged form of theological liberalism that

---

[8] Livingston, *Modern Christian Thought*, 262.

[9] Livingston, *Modern Christian Thought*, 356-370.

reigned in the early 20th century. His is indeed an old kind of Christianity.

ON HUMAN NATURE & SIN

McLaren first provided hints to his theological understanding of human nature and sin in an early work, *The Story We Find Ourselves In*, which he later developed in *A New Kind of Christianity*. In this second part of his *New Kind of Christian* trilogy, McLaren establishes the framing narrative for his new kind of Christian, one that would eventually form the foundation for his new kind of Christianity. Through his protagonist Neo, McLaren contends that the modern telling of the Christian story has been distorted, because it imported "the Greek idea of a fall from a perfect, unchanging, ideal, complete, harmonious, fully formed world into a world of change, challenge, conflict..." [10]   For McLaren, there was no fall, in the traditional sense of the historic doctrine of sin. Instead, "the God-given goodness in creation isn't lost...God's creative fingerprint or signature is still there, always and forever. The evil of humanity doesn't eradicate the goodness of God's creation, even though it puts all of that goodness at risk." [11] Instead of creating a perfect world that "falls" from a Platonic perfect ideal, it is "a story of emergence;" creation is evolutionary and "must go on

---

[10] Brian McLaren, *The Story We Find Ourselves In* (San Francisco: Jossey-Bass, 2003), 52. This is later affirmed and further developed in *A New Kind of Christianity*, 33-45.

[11] McLaren, *Story We Find Ourselves*, 52.

creating itself." [12] Therefore, humanity has not fallen and is still good. This initial exploration of McLaren's view of Creation and the Fall is important when we begin exploring his understanding of humanity and sin.

As the Earth's story is one of emergence, so too is humanity's; our story is not a fall from perfection into a state of imperfection, but "unfolds as a kind of compassionate...classic coming-of-age story." [13] While the traditional doctrine of the Fall contends "there is one cataclysmic event in which the first humans descend—or fall, if you will—from their ideal, perfect state into the material, imperfect story of history," McLaren does not see just one single cataclysmic crisis but "an avalanche of crises" that:

> all involve human beings gaining levels of intellectual and technological development that surpass their moral development—people becoming too smart, too powerful for their own good...Human beings leave their identity, their life, their story as creatures in God's creation...As they become more independent, they lose their connection to God, their sense of dependence...So they experience alienation from God." [14]

---

[12] McLaren, *Story We Find Ourselves*, 52. In fact, in *A New Kind of Christianity* McLaren asserts, "Evolution fits beautifully in the good world of Elohim." 267n.4.

[13] McLaren, *New Kind of Christianity*, 49, 51.

[14] McLaren, *Story We Find Ourselves*, 53-54, 56.

In other words, as humans "come of age" they grow beyond God, and their relationship deteriorates in progressive, fi tful "experiences of alienation." McLaren describes this progress and growth in his book, *The Secret Message of Jesus* in this way:

> [Adam's and Eve's] noble status quickly deteriorates as they disconnect from God and reject any limits placed upon their freedom by their Creator. The results of their disobedience are visible as the story unfolds—a sense of shame and alienation from God and one another, violence of brother against brother, disharmony with creation itself, misunderstanding and conflict among tribes and nations. [15]

For McLaren, there is no event of "the Fall" or corresponding "original sin" and "total depravity" in which humanity plunged into rebellion and alienation, resulting in an inherited sinful nature. [16]   Instead, the framing narrative of humanity is one of systemic progression and ascent, with corresponding descent resulting in "new depths of moral evil and social injustice." [17]   In his re-imagined framing narrative, individuals are no longer the issue, but the human systems; "socioeconomic and technological advances" lead to moral evil and social

---

[15]   Brian McLaren, *The Secret Message of Jesus* (Nashville: Word Publishing, 2006), 27.

[16] McLaren, *The Secret Message of Jesus*, 27.

[17] McLaren, *New Kind of Christianity*, 51.

injustice, not individuals acting upon their sinful nature. [18] In the words of McLaren, "it's a story about the downside of 'progress'—a story of human foolishness...the human turn toward rebellion...the human intention toward evil." [19] The problem isn't that humans rebelled against God and are rebels or that humans did evil and are evil. For McLaren, the story is one of humans creating evil and damaging and savaging God's good world, it is a story where "humans have evil intent," instead of being evil themselves. Th ose evil intentions are not the result of an evil heart, but the bad systems and stories that consume humans.

This framing narrative fi rst written in *The Story We Find Ourselves In* evolved into a later work in which McLaren addresses the big questions and problems that face our world, insisting that everything must change. In his similarly titled book, *Everything Must Change*, McLaren believes the main dysfunctions of humanity are ethical; he frames the crisis of the human condition as a crisis of prosperity, equity, and security. [20] Th ese three crises form the "cogs" in what McLaren terms the *suicide machine*. [21] The suicide machine is a metaphor for "the systems that drive our civilization toward un-health and un-peace." [22] McLaren envisions the driving force behind our broken,

---

[18] McLaren, *New Kind of Christianity*, 51.

[19] McLaren, *New Kind of Christianity*, 54.

[20] Brian McLaren, *Everything Must Change* (Nashville: Thomas Nelson Publishers, 2007), 5.

[21] McLaren, *Everything Must Change*, 53.

[22] McLaren, *Everything Must Change*, 53. (emphasis mine)

problematic condition to reside in the systems of the world, rather than in the individual person. According to him, humanity suffers from a "dysfunction of our societal machinery," which is operated not by single individuals but by humanity acting together." [23] In other words, individual sinful human nature is not the problem, but rather a universal sin of society,

Primarily, the dysfunction and sin of society is measured by our collective framing story. No matter what group we belong to, we are under the influence of that group's framing story, where we learn our origin, our destination, and how we should act in between along the way. According to McLaren, our world's dominant framing story is failing for three main reasons: it does not "guide us to respect environmental limits, but instead inspires pursuit of as much resource use and waste production as possible," resulting in an unsustainable way of life; it does not "lead us to work for the common good," but instead encourage each group to become "a competing us/them faction that seeks advantage for 'us,' not a common good for all;" and "our framing story does not lead these competing factions to reconcile peacefully," instead locking our world "in a vicious cycle of tension between an anxious global empire of the rich and an angry global terrorist revolution of the poor." [24]

In *A New Kind of Christianity*, McLaren illustrates this explanation of the human condition and reality of so-called "social sin." Using the story of the Israelites in Exodus, he

---

[23] McLaren, *Everything Must Change*, 65.

[24] McLaren, *Everything Must Change*, 68-70.

explains that it is a story of "liberation from the external oppression of social sin," while also celebrating "liberation from the internal spiritual oppression of personal sin." Because McLaren does not believe that sin is part of human nature because of an event of rebellion, he must mean something different by "internal spiritual oppression of personal sin."[25] It seems even this internal oppression is related to the social systems of sin, because he asserts that people are freed from "the *dominating powers* of fear, greed, impatience, ingratitude, and so on." [26] The power of Fear and Ingratitude, then are the oppressors, which in the Exodus narrative apparently results from years of being "debased by generations of slavery." [27] This slave framing story, then, is what contributed to the Israelites communal and individual commitment to "fear, greed, impatience, ingratitude, and so on." The internal compulsion toward greed, for example, was an internal power that resulted from the external system of slavery and the bad framing narrative out of which Israel was liberated. Thus, our ultimate problem is bad systems and stories.

Unlike the traditional historic faith that locates the problem of the human condition in individual sinfulness and an inherited sinful nature, McLaren believes humans are in trouble because we are in bondage to the "dominant societal machinery," which entices us to keep faith in its systems of wealthy, security, pleasure, and injustice. [28] This

---

[25] McLaren, *New Kind of Christianity*, 58.

[26] McLaren, *New Kind of Christianity*, 58. (emphasis mine.)

[27] McLaren, *New Kind of Christianity*, 58.

[28] McLaren, *Everything Must Change*, 271.

faith and bondage has led to a sort of universal consciousness that is driven by destructive, dysfunctional framing stories. Th e global crises of which McLaren says we must be saved are the symptoms and consequences of the dysfunction, resulting in a collection of human evil. Dysfunctional societal machinery, destructive framing narratives, and collective human evil are our problems. They compel innately good humans to act badly, rather than in inner, natural compulsion.

McLaren's understanding of the human condition and sin fi nds several points of connection to the theology of Ritschl. First, McLaren reflects Ritschl's own rejection of the historic doctrine of original sin. In confronting the idea of original sin, Ritschl relegates it to the sphere of "doctrine," insisting it is an intellectual idea that does not conform to experience. [29] Like McLaren, Ritschl rejects the notion that there was both an original righteousness and fall from that original constitution. [30] In fact, the doctrine of original sin that developed in the early church and was codified by Augustine out of this assumption [31] is challenged by Ritschl to in no way reflect any New Testament authors: "Neither Jesus nor any of the New

---

[29] Albrecht Ritschl, *The Christian Doctrine of Justification and Reconciliation: The Positive Development of the Doctrine*. Edited by H.R. Mackintosh and A.B. Macaulay (Edinburgh: T & T Clark, 1902.), 328.

[30] Ritschl, *Justification and Reconciliation*, 331.

[31] Albrect Ritschl, *Instruction in the Christian Religion*. Translated by Alice Mead Wing (London: Longmans, Green & Co, 1901), 203.n27. Here he writes, "Augustine's doctrine of original sin, ie., that the original inclination to evil transmitted in generation is for every one both personal guilt and subject to the divine sentence of eternal punishment, is not confirmed by any New Testament author."

Testament writers either indicate or presuppose that sin is universal merely through natural generation." [32] Likewise, he disputed as unbiblical the Reformed assertion that humans are incapable of doing good because of their inherent sinfulness. [33] Furthermore, Ritschl argued that original sin is neither derived from the natural endowment of man [34] nor inherited from previous generations. [35] Instead, Ritschl argued that sin is acquired through human history and development.

McLaren describes such an acquisition by asserting that the human narrative as one that is a "classic coming of age story." In other words, the condition of humanity evolved. Instead of inheriting a sinful nature from Adam, the generations from our first human parents got trapped in an "avalanche of crises" that engulfed humanity in dysfunctional systems and destructive stories. In the words of Ritschl, humanity is now caught in a "whole web of sinful actions and reaction, which presuppose and yet again increases the selfish bias in every man." [36] Humans were created with the capacity to freely direct their impulses toward the "perfect common good" or highest good. [37] From the beginning humans were created with an internal goodness that was to be directed toward the

---

[32] Ritschl, *Instruction in the Christian Religion*, 203.n27.

[33] Ritschl, *Instruction in the Christian Religion*, 206-207.n4.

[34] Ritschl, *Instruction in the Christian Religion*, 204.

[35] Ritschl, *Justification and Reconciliation*, 348.

[36] Ritschl, *Justification and Reconciliation*, 350.

[37] Ritschl, *Instruction in the Christian Religion*, 202.

highest common good, which the Kingdom of God reflects. Now we are caught in webs similar to McLaren's dysfunctional systems and destructive stories that have escalated over time, webs which compel every man toward selfish acts.

Was it inevitable that humans would use their freedom to choose the opposite of the common good? Ritschl wrote that "The possibility and probability of sinning...can be derived from the fact that the human will...is a constantly growing power whose activity also is not from the fi rst accompanied by a complete knowledge of the good." [38] Like McLaren's assertion that human power grew and developed over time from hunter-gatherers to empire dwellers, Ritschl suggests that the capacity for humans to act grew and developed over time, which inevitably led to an abuse of freedom. Th is freedom from our first parents resulted in a "defect in reverence and in trust in God, or indifference and mistrust of Him," which is the basic form of their sin.[39] In other words they lost "their connection to God, their sense of dependence...So they experienced alienation from God." [40]

In Adam, there is a universal loss of connection, dependence, reverence, and trust in God, because every generation has actively participated in the transgression of freely mistrusting God and rejecting the perfect moral good. Th ese collective acts have resulted in what Ritschl calls the "kingdom of sin" or "web of sin." For Ritschl, the

---

[38] Ritschl, *Instruction in the Christian Religion*, 204.

[39] Ritschl, *Justification and Reconciliation*, 334.

[40] McLaren, *Story We Find Ourselves*, 56.

kingdom of sin is an alternative hypothesis to original sin that explains the human condition. [41] This kingdom or universal sinfulness is the collective human sins that act as a collective conscious out of which individuals act. He also describes this kingdom and universality as "united action" which leads to a reenforcement of sin in every generation: "United sin, this opposite of the kingdom of God, rests upon all as a power which at least limits the freedom of the individual to do good." [42] Like McLaren's dysfunctional systems and destructive stories, the sin that swirls around us compels us to sin, which cashes out as a sinful bias that is acquired by individuals because of bad examples. As Ritschl explains, "The sinful bias...is not described by [Paul] as inherited, and can with perfect reason be understood as something acquired. In the individual [the sinful bias] comes to be the principle of the will's direction."[43] This individual bias contributes to the larger whole of "wickedness and untruth" in what Ritschl terms a "web of sinful action." It is the collective contribution of individual actions and reactions and also "increases the selfish bias in every man." [44] This "web of sin" is the dysfunctional systems and destructive stories of which McLaren speaks.

Both McLaren and Ritschl believe our human problem is what we do and not who we are by nature—we do not sin because we're sinners; we are a sinner because we sin in

---

[41] McLaren, *Story We Find Ourselves*, 56.

[42] Ritschl, *Instruction in the Christian Religion*, 206.

[43] Ritschl, *Justification and Reconciliation*, 346, 347.

[44] Ritschl, *Justification and Reconciliation*, 350.

concert with humanity and its web of sin. The web of sin that surrounds us creates a bias within us toward selfishness and compels us to sin; we are oppressed on the outside not affected on the inside. Therefore, our solution must address this evil web of systems, the person who came to bring us that solution had to do something with that web. We didn't need a savior to stand in our place of punishment; we needed someone to launch a better system, a better Kingdom.

ON THE PERSON & WORK OF CHRIST

If our human problem is the dysfunctional societal machinery and destructive framing narratives—in other words the "web of sin" and bad ethics formed by the world's systems and stories—what is the solution? For McLaren Jesus is indeed the answer for the world today, but in a way that is different from historical Christian orthodoxy. While the historic Christian faith recognizes Jesus Christ as God and in some way a penal substitute sacrifice for the sins of the world, McLaren recognizes neither. Instead, Jesus is merely the best teacher of a better way of living, the one who lived the best way to be human, and one who is our best picture of the character of God. The best teacher, way, and picture of God is the perfect solution to McLaren's problem, because according to him we need a better example to follow in order to live differently and avert dysfunction and destruction. In *The Story We Find Ourselves In*, McLaren describes Jesus as a "revolutionary" who was a "master of living". [45] According

---

[45] McLaren, *Story We Find Ourselves*, 115, 121, 122.

to McLaren, "Jesus really is in some mysterious and in a unique way sent from God and full of God." [46]   Notice McLaren does not say Jesus *is* God, but merely a messenger of sorts from God and *full* of Him, which is code for sharing in the divine. As it will be shown, His fellowship with God comes from his ethical way of living; He is the moral, not the metaphysical, Son of God. While McLaren doesn't outright deny His ontological divinity, he never says He is God Himself, either. Again, because the problem is bad systems and stories, our solution needed to be in the form of a better teaching, system, way of life, and story. Jesus provides that new, better system and story as a messenger from God who founds His Kingdom.

McLaren affirms this characterization in his recent book by insisting that Jesus "brings us to a new evolutionary level in our understanding of God...the experience of God in Jesus requires a brand-new definition or understanding of God," because He "gives us the highest, deepest, and most mature view of the character of the living God." [47] This emphasis on the "character of God" is used throughout McLaren's description of the person of God in *A New Kind of Christianity*: "When you see [Jesus], you are getting the best view afforded to humans of the character of God;" "Jesus serves as the Word-made-flesh revelation of the character of God;" and "the invisible God has been made visible in his life. 'If you want to know what God is like,' Jesus says, 'look at me, my life, my ways, my

---

[46] McLaren, *Story We Find Ourselves*, 122.

[47] McLaren, *New Kind of Christianity*, 114, 115.

deeds, my character.'" [48]   Elsewhere he writes, that Jesus simply identifies Himself *with* God, telling His disciples that those who had seen Him had in "some real way" also seen God. [49] In fact, McLaren agrees with a Quaker scholar, Elton Trueblood, whom he quotes: "The historic Christian doctrine of the divinity of Christ does not simply mean that Jesus is like God. It is far more radical than that. It means that God is like Jesus." [50]   Jesus, then, is not God Himself: Jesus is like God and God is like Jesus. In a "mysterious and unique way" Jesus is full of God. He shows, images and expresses God's character. McLaren suggests He accomplishes this primarily through his life and teachings. Th is is a good thing because humanity needs a better life and set of teachings.

From McLaren's earlier writings one can detect this theological trajectory and emphasis on Jesus as "teacher" and "liver." In explaining Jesus as "Lord," he argues this means Jesus "was the master of living...it would mean that no one else could take the raw materials of life...and elicit from them a beautiful song of truth and goodness. [The disciples] believed Jesus' way was higher and more brilliant, and the right way to launch a revolution of God." [51] Elsewhere he writes that Jesus' message and teachings is an "alternative framing story" that can "save the system from suicide," a message that focuses "on personal, social, and

---

[48] McLaren, *New Kind of Christianity*, 118, 128, 222.

[49] McLaren, *Secret Message of Jesus*, 31.

[50] As quoted by McLaren, *New Kind of Christianity*, 114.

[51] McLaren, *The Story We Find Ourselves In*, 121.

global transformation in this life." [52] Furthermore, "Jesus' life and message centered on the articulation and demonstration of a radically different framing story—one that critiques and exposes the imperial narratives as dangerous to itself and others." [53] Again, since the problem is bad systems and stories, Jesus' mastery over life through his higher, brilliant way of living and alternative message provides the existential solution to our existential problem.

What exactly was that message that Jesus articulated? The message of the Kingdom of God, or as McLaren puts it the "revolution of God." Th rough his life and teachings, Jesus "inserted into human history a seed of grace, truth, and hope that can never be defeated," a seed that will "prevail over the evil and injustice of humanity and lead to the world's ongoing transformation into the world God dreams of." [54] Because the human problem is bad systems and stories, we need a new system and a new story to repair and heal us. Jesus provides humanity the solution through his teachings on the Kingdom of God and living out the way of that Kingdom. McLaren makes it clear that the central point of Jesus is the Kingdom of God. As he insists, "[Jesus] came to launch a new Genesis, to lead a new Exodus, and to announce, embody, and inaugurate a new kingdom as the Prince of Peace. Seen in this light, Jesus and his message has everything to do with poverty, slavery, and a 'social agenda.'" [55] He insists that Jesus himself "saw

---

[52] McLaren, *Everything Must Change*, 73, 22.

[53] McLaren, *Everything Must Change*, 154-155.

[54] McLaren, *Everything Must Change*, 79-80.

[55] McLaren, *New Kind of Christianity*, 135.

these dynamics at work in his day and proposed in word and deed a new alternative. Jesus' creative and transforming framing story invited people to change the world by disbelieving old framing stories and believing a new one: a story about a loving God who calls all people to live life in a new way." [56]

His newest book revises and extends these arguments by insisting that Jesus came to "lead the way in liberation from the social and spiritual oppression of his day;" He was chosen by God "to liberate His people from oppression." [57] As we have already seen, our human problem is not a sinful nature, but dysfunctional systems and destructive stories. Rather than being affected on the inside by a sinful nature, we are oppressed on the outside by bad social and spiritual systems and stories. Jesus is the antidote, the cure for these bad systems and stories by providing the alternative system and story of the Kingdom through His life and teachings. And what is the Kingdom of God? "A life that is radically different from the way people are living these days, a life that is full and over flowing, a higher life that is centered in an interactive relationship with God and with Jesus...an extraordinary life to the full centered on a relationship with God." [58] According to McLaren, this is what the Apostle John termed "eternal life," or "life of the ages." Through his Kingdom message and Kingdom way of living, "Jesus is promising a life that transcends 'life in the present age'... [he] is offering a life in the new Genesis, the new creation

---

[56] McLaren, *Everything Must Change*, 237-274.

[57] McLaren, *New Kind of Christianity*, 131, 132.

[58] McLaren, *Secret Message of Jesus*, 37.

that is 'of the age' not simply part of the current regimes, plots, kingdoms, and economies created by humans." [59] Jesus has come, then, to liberate us from these old regimes (i.e. dysfunctional systems) and plots (i.e. destructive stories) and teach and show us the highest, best way found in the Kingdom. As liberator from the bad systems and stories of the world, this course of action culminates in the ultimate showdown between the system and story of Caesar and Christ: the cross.

In the traditional Christian faith, the cross occupies a central feature of God's saving plan and work of Christ, for upon it Christ breaks open his body and sheds his blood for our sins in our stead as a substitute. What place does the cross have in McLaren's Christology? As with the other parts of his theology, the cross does have a place in God's saving movement, but a different one from the historic understanding. In response to the existing theories of the atoning work of Christ he argues for what he terms the 'powerful weakness theory,' which hinges on the word vulnerable:

> by becoming vulnerable on the cross, by accepting suffering from everyone...Jesus is showing God's loving heart, which wants forgiveness, not revenge, for everyone. Jesus shows us that the wisdom of God's kingdom is sacrifice, not violence. It's about accepting suffering and transforming it into reconciliation, not avenging suffering through retaliation. So through this window, the cross shows God's rejection of the human violence and dominance

---

[59] McLaren, *New Kind of Christianity*, 130.

and oppression that have spun the world in a cycle of crisis..." [60]

Later he insists that "the cross calls humanity to stop trying to make God's Kingdom happen through coercion and force...and instead to welcome it through self-sacrifice and vulnerability." [61] For McLaren, the cross is a stage upon which Christ renders a grand performance illustrating God's love, wisdom, acceptance, and new way of sacrifice and suffering. Through the cross Jesus "exposes Roman violence and religious complicity, while pronouncing a sentence of forgiveness on his crucifiers." Throughout Jesus' life, his message has been one of non-violence and triumph over enemies through peace and self-sacrifice. The cross, then, is the culmination of those teachings as an exposé on love. Rather than joining in with the "'shock and awe' display of power as Roman crucifixions were intended to do," Jesus gives us a "'reverence and awe' display of God's willingness to accept rejection and mistreatment..." [62] The cross is not the point at which God objectively dealt with the objective reality of human sin and our sin nature, as the historic faith insists. Instead, the cross event gave us the example of love, self-sacrifice, peace, and way of God's alternative Kingdom in contrast to the prevailing system and story of Rome.

Like his views on the human sinful condition, McLaren mirrors Ritschl's Christology in significant ways, too.

---

[60] McLaren, *The Story We Find Ourselves In*, 105. (emphasis mine.)

[61] McLaren, *The Story We Find Ourselves In*, 106.

[62] McLaren, *New Kind of Christianity*, 158-159.

According to Ritschl, "Jesus, the Founder of the perfect moral and spiritual religion, belongs to a higher order than all other men;" "His unique worth lies in the manner in which He mastered His spiritual powers through a self-consciousness which transcends that of all other men..." [63] As a unique higher man, He was "conscious of a new and hitherto unknown relation to God." [64] As with McLaren, Ritschl does not describe Jesus as being God himself, only a unique man belonging to a higher order of humanity. In fact, in regard to his relationship with God Jesus is described as having a *strength of a fellowship or unity with God* such as no one before Him had ever known." [65] Apparently, Jesus' "unity" with God is similar to the fellowship or unity a man has with his wife: he and she are not ontologically one, they simply possess a relationship with each other unlike anyone else they have had with another. For Ritschl the same is true of Jesus with God: Jesus is not ontologically one with God, but simply has a unique relationship with Him. This uniqueness cashes out in his higher ethical display through his life and teachings.

We see a fuller picture of the theological connections between their Christology by exploring how Ritschl describes Jesus' divinity. Like McLaren Ritschl does not indicate Jesus is God, but instead Jesus "brings the perfect revelation of God, so that beyond what He brings no further revelation is conceivable or is to be looked for;" He

---

[63] Ritschl, *Justification and Reconciliation*, 2, 332.

[64] Ritschl, *Justification and Reconciliation*, 386.

[65] Ritschl, *Justification and Reconciliation*, 333. (emphasis mine)

is the "Bearer of the final revelation of God." [66] In Jesus we also see "the complete revelation of God as love, grace, and faithfulness." [67] It is when we examine the life of Christ that we receive this image of God and come to a fuller understanding of His person: "when we have placed the one common material of Christ's life, His speech and conduct as well as his patience in suffering...we exhaust the significance of his person as Bearer of the Divine lordship, or founder of the Divine Kingdom." [68]   As McLaren suggests, Jesus is the highest, most advanced view of God and His character. Both McLaren and Ritschl agree that through Jesus' life we see and experience God. They believe Jesus shares in the Divine and is "full of God" because of how he acted, not who he was.

Furthermore, Christ's ethical actions are what connect him to God and give him what Ritschl terms the attribute of Godhead and Godhood. "Christ's Godhead is understood as the power which Christ has put forth for our redemption...[the Godhead attribute] of Christ is to be found in the service He provided, the benefit He bestows, the saving work He accomplishes...it is an attribute revealed to us in His saving influence upon ourselves." [69]   Christ is God because of what He does, not who He is. Jesus is not ontologically God, but ethically so: He shares in the Divine because of His ethical services and action. In the words of McLaren, "Jesus is in some mysterious and unique

---

[66] Ritschl, *Justification and Reconciliation*, 388, 397.

[67] Ritschl, *Instruction in the Christian Religion*, 197.

[68] Ritschl, *Justification and Reconciliation*, 482-483.

[69] Ritschl, *Justification and Reconciliation*, 395, 396-397, 398.

way...full of God." Jesus is not God, but uniquely participates in the Divine through his higher ethical living and teaching.

As Ritschl makes clear, it is through the ethical activity of Jesus we find God. While Ritschl does say "[Jesus] is equal to God," it is clear from his writings that this equality is ethical, rather than ontological. He is equal with God because of his moral and ethical activity. [70] This activity is primarily the fulfillment of his vocation as the founder of the Kingdom. As Ritschl asserts, Jesus is the "personal vehicle of the Divine self-end;" He is "that Being in the world Whose self-end God makes effective and manifest after the original manner His own eternal self-end, Whose whole activity, therefore, in discharge of His vocation, forms the material of that complete revelation of God which is present in Him, in Whom, in short, the Word of God is a human person." [71] Jesus reveals God through His vocation as the founder of the Kingdom of God, as a "teacher" and "liver" of the "universal ethical kingdom of God," which is the "supreme end of God Himself in the world." [72] Jesus' ethical teachings and kingdom vocation, then, constitute Him as participating in the "Godhead," in the Divine. In fact, his "Divine" authority as Ruler does not come from being God Himself, but "by His morally effective teaching and by His gracious mode of conduct..."[73]

---

[70] Ritschl, *Justification and Reconciliation*, 483.

[71] Ritschl, *Justification and Reconciliation*, 451.

[72] Ritschl, *Justification and Reconciliation*, 451.

[73] Ritschl, *Instruction in the Christian Religion*, 195.

Finally, the significance of the work of Jesus is "'related to the moral organization of humanity through love-prompted action," [74] which is the Kingdom of God. His vocation was founding, living, and teaching the love-prompted actions of the Kingdom as triumph and transcendence over the ethically bad systems of the world. Through this vocation he provided the prototypical example of self-sacrifice, discipline, and attainment of virtue for others to follow. This was especially acute through His work on the cross, which served as confirmation and codification of that vocation for the rest of the world. Ritschl argued—which McLaren himself later affirmed and recycled—that the significance of Jesus' work on the cross for others served as an example to the rest of the world: "It is not mere fate of dying that determines the value of Christ's death as a sacrifice; what renders this issue of his life significant for others is His willing acceptance of the death inflicted on Him by His adversaries as a dispensation of God, and the highest proof of faithfulness to His vocation." [75] Thus, His sufferings served as a means of testing His faithfulness to His vocation, while also confirming and codifying it. [76] Both Ritschl and McLaren affirm that the work of Christ centered on founding, living, and teaching the Kingdom, and the cross was the culmination of that vocation in that this highest ethical common good was tested and displayed for all the world to see and follow, which is where we find our salvation.

---

[74] Ritschl, *Justification and Reconciliation*, 13.

[75] Ritschl, *Justification and Reconciliation*, 477, 4779

[76] Ritschl, *Justification and Reconciliation*, 480.

ON SALVATION

As this examination has already illustrated, Ritschl and McLaren believe our problem is the dysfunctional systems and destructive stories of our world. Our solution came when God called Jesus as a messenger to show a better way of living and teach a better story: the Kingdom system and Kingdom story. McLaren and Ritschl agree that he is the vehicle of the Divine because of the way he lived and taught. Through his vocation as founder of the Kingdom of God Jesus was filled with God—meaning He acted like God would act on earth—and ultimately revealed the character of God. In so acting and revealing he is the vehicle for an existential solution to our existential problem. McLaren has written of his journey toward better understanding the dynamics of this solution. Perhaps this theological exploration was most expressed in Everything Must Change when he asked, "Is Jesus' healing and transforming framing story really powerful enough to save the world?" [77] Because McLaren believes our systems and stories are the problem, our solution is found in an alternative system and story, which we find in Jesus' message on the Kingdom of God. McLaren answers his question on the following page:

> if we believe that God graciously offers us a new way, a new truth, and a new life, we can be liberated from the vicious, addictive cycles of our suicidal framing stories. That kind of faith will save us...our failure to believe [Jesus' good news] will keep us from experiencing its saving

---

[77] McLaren, *Everything Must Change*, 269.

potential, and so we'll spin on in the vicious cycles of Caesar. [78]

According to McLaren, our salvation is found in being liberated from the systems and stories of the world and believing in the new system and story—the new way, truth, and life—found in Jesus' teachings on the Kingdom. We find salvation when we "transfer our trust from the way of Caesar to the way of Christ." [79] Notice that McLaren doesn't call people to trust Christ Himself, but instead trust the *way of Christ*. McLaren urges us to transfer our trust from the world's systems and stories—represented by Caesar—to the system and story of Christ, which is the Kingdom of God. Ultimately, salvation is participation in the Kingdom of God, which he calls *participatory eschatology*.

While conventional eschatologies have cultivated "resignation, fear, and arrogant aggression," participatory eschatology inspires "a passion to do good, whatever the suffering, sacrifice, and delay because of a confidence that God will win in the end; courage, because God's Spirit is at work in the world and what God begins God will surely bring to completion; a sense of urgency, because we are protagonists in a story; and humility and kindness, because we are aware of our ability to miss the point, lose our way, and play on the wrong side." [80]   In fact, the death and resurrection of Jesus are paradigms for this salvation in which we ourselves are to participate in anticipation of this

---

[78] McLaren, *Everything Must Change*, 270.

[79] McLaren, *Everything Must Change*, 271.

[80] McLaren, *New Kind of Christianity*, 200.

coming Kingdom: we join with Jesus in dying (metaphorically to our pride and agendas, literally in martyrdom as a witness to God's Kingdom and justice); and rising again in triumph "through the mysterious but real power of God. In this cruciform way, we participate in the ongoing work of God, and we anticipate its ultimate success." [81] For McLaren, our dying and rising with Christ are symbolic of our rejection of and triumph over the dysfunctional systems and destructive stories of our world. Salvation comes not from dying to the old sinful nature by believing in Jesus' death and rising to new life by believing in his resurrection. Instead, we are called to die to the bad ethics of the world and rise to new life by living like Jesus. Thus, salvation is entirely existential, in that His loving example is what saves us from our bad existence, an existential salvation that extends to the whole human race.

Because we are called to live in the system and story of the Kingdom by living the teachings of Jesus, ultimate salvation at judgment will be based on behavior, not beliefs. "God will examine the story of our lives for signs of Christlikeness...These are the parts of a person's life that will be deemed worthy of being saved, remembered, rewarded, and raised to new beginnings." [82] Rather than believing in Jesus' sacrifice on the cross and God resurrecting the Son, giving food and water to the needy, showing mercy, welcoming the stranger, and being generous like Jesus is what God cares about, what will lead to salvation. Conversely, "all the unloving, unjust, non-

---

[81] McLaren, *New Kind of Christianity*, 200-201.

[82] McLaren, *New Kind of Christianity*, 204.

Christlike parts of our lives...will be burned away, counted as unworthy, condemned, and forgotten forever." [83] In the end ultimate salvation is dependent upon our ethics, whether we walk the path of Jesus in word and deed. Since "no good deed will be forgotten," we are urged to "start doing the next good thing now and never give up until the dream comes true," until God's Kingdom comes. [84] Human salvation is not found in the broken body and shed blood on the cross, but in the new system and story of the Kingdom coming to earth as founded by Jesus' life and teachings.

It is important to note that the cross carries little soteriological significance for McLaren beyond pointing to an example of love and suffering in the face of the oppressive system and story of Caesar. [85] In fact, in his counter narrative to the traditional view of the cross—which maintains "God sent Jesus into the world to absorb all the punishment for our sins" [86] —one of McLaren's characters insists this view "sounds like divine child abuse," [87] as if God the Father was abusing His Son on the cross. Instead, the cross is about Jesus' vulnerability and accepting suffering, showing God's loving heart, and showing us that Kingdom sacrifice is not violent but

---

[83] McLaren, *New Kind of Christianity*, 204.

[84] McLaren, *Everything Must Change*, 146.

[85] In fact, in the part of *A New Kind of Christianity* that is designed to answer the *Narrative Questions* (Ch. 4-6) the event of the cross is neither emphasized nor mentioned.

[86] McLaren, *Story We Find Ourselves*, 101.

[87] McLaren, *Story We Find Ourselves*, 102.

reconciliation through suffering. [88] For McLaren, salvation comes when we follow Jesus' example of non-violent vulnerability and suffering, which culminated at the cross.

His view of salvation agrees with the theologian Jürgen Moltmann, whom he quotes: "The one [Jesus] will triumph who first died for the victims and then also the executioners, and in so doing revealed a new righteousness which breaks through the vicious circles of hate and vengeance and which, from the victims and executioners, creates...a new humanity." [89] This view does not stem from the apostle Paul's, which viewed the death and resurrection of Christ revealing a new righteousness from God that comes through faith in that death and resurrection. [90] Likewise, a new humanity is not born out of the defeat of sin through death and the resurrection, as Paul argues. [91] Instead, this new righteousness and new humanity is ethical; salvation from the dysfunctional systems and destructive stories comes because of Jesus' acts of love in the face of hate and suffering in the face of vengeance. Likewise, an alternative community is born through similar ethical acts of love and suffering; a new humanity happens when people participate in the righteous ethic of Jesus.

Like McLaren, Ritschl rejects the traditional substitutionary view of the cross as providing the means of salvation for humanity: "The view that Christ, by the

---

[88] McLaren, *Story We Find Ourselves*, 105.

[89] Jürgen Moltmann, *The Crucified God* (London: SCM, 1974), 178. As quoted in McLaren, *New Kind of Christianity*, 206

[90] See Rm. 3:21-26.

[91] Rm. 5:12-20.

vicarious endurance of the punishment deserved by sinful men, propitiated the justice or wrath of God, and thus made possible the grace of God, is not found on any clear and distinct passage in the New Testament." [92]   And like McLaren, Ritschl does not believe the solution to man's problem of alienation comes through faith in the substitution of Christ on the cross. Instead, salvation comes through attaining the Kingdom of God. According to Ritschl, "The kingdom of God is the divinely vouched-for highest good of the community...the ethical ideal for whose attainment the members of the community bind themselves together through their definite reciprocal action." [93]   Ritschl explicitly claims that the Kingdom of God is the solution to the problem of mankind when he writes:

> [the kingdom of God] offers the solution to the question propounded or implied in all religions: namely, how man, recognizing himself as a part of the world, and at the same time as being capable of a spiritual personality, can attain that dominion over the world, as opposed to limitation by it, which this capability gives him the right to claim. [94]

Here Ritschl reveals that the problem is very similar to McLaren's: humanity must rise above the world, which is the bad systems and stories. In fact, "A universal ethical

---

[92] Ritschl, *Instruction in the Christian Religion*, 220.n3.

[93] Ritschl, *Instruction in the Christian Religion*, 174-175.

[94] Ritschl, *Instruction in the Christian Religion*, 179.

Kingdom of God is the supreme end of God Himself in the world," [95] and thus the end toward which all of humanity is to move. This movement toward attaining the ethical ideal of the Kingdom is possible through the justification Christ provides, two concepts which are in reality one in the same.

While others often separate justification and the Kingdom of God, claiming that "justification and reconciliation concern men as sinners, while the Kingdom of God concerns them as reconciled," Ritschl insists this dichotomy is "not quite exact." [96] Instead, "the conception of the Kingdom of God and justification are homogeneous," they are one and the same idea. [97] The aim of justification and reconciliation is "lordship over the world;" justification is transcending and moving beyond the systems and stories of the world through "dominion over the world and participation in the Kingdom of God."[98] Thus, it appears as though we are the ones who justify ourselves. Though McLaren doesn't frame it in terms of justification and reconciliation—that would be too similar to a Reformed framing—he does insist we need deliverance from the world as Ritschl does. As Ritschl defines reconciliation: "[it] is not merely the ground of deliverance from the guilt of sin...it is also the ground of deliverance from the world, and the ground of spiritual and moral

[95] Ritschl, *Justification and Reconciliation*, 451.

[96] Ritschl, *Justification and Reconciliation*, 31.

[97] Ritschl, *Justification and Reconciliation*, 33.

[98] Ritschl, *Justification and Reconciliation*, 609, 628.

lordship over the world." [99]   Rather than deliverance from the condition of sin, we receive deliverance from the effects of sin. Th is is further emphasized when Ritschl claims justification leads to eternal life now, "which is present in our experiences of freedom or lordship over the world, and in the independence of self-feeling both from the restrictions and from the impulses due to natural causes or particular sections of society." [100]

That Kingdom is the product of "love-inspired action" and "the righteous conduct in which the members of the Christian community share in the bringing in of the kingdom of God [which] has its universal law and its personal motive in love to God and to one's neighbor." [101] The Kingdom is not the eschatological reign of God per se that will restore the world from the ontological consequences of sin, but rather the "moral society of nations" and ultimately "the organization of humanity through action inspired by love." [102]   Salvation, then, is found by aligning one's life with the teachings and way of Jesus and participating in his own vocation as the prototype of a life of love, and liberation and elevation from the worldly motives, systems, and stories. [103] Similarly, McLaren exclusively emphasizes a salvation from the systems and stories of the world through aligning one's

---

[99] Ritschl, *Justification and Reconciliation*, 357.

[100] Ritschl, *Justification and Reconciliation*, 534-534.

[101] Ritschl, *Instruction in the Christian Religion*, 178, 174.

[102] Ritschl, *Justification and Reconciliation*, 10, 12.

[103] Ritschl, *Justification and Reconciliation*, 469.

life with Christ and participation in the ethical, earthly Kingdom of God. Our existential problem is solved not through belief in the substitutionary sacrifice of Jesus Christ on the cross and his defeat of death through the resurrection, but instead good behavior and ethical deliverance from the world.

CONCLUSION

This historical comparative examination has sought to examine and compare elements of McLaren's theology to Ritschl along three lines of reasoning: the problem of sin, the person and work of Christ, and solution of salvation. In concluding this examination, perhaps Ritschl's theology is best summarized by his definition of Christianity:

> Christianity, then, is the monotheistic, completely spiritual and ethical religion, which, based on the life of its Author as Redeemer and Founder of the Kingdom of God, consists in the freedom of the children of God, involves the impulse to conduct from the motive of love, which aims at the moral organization of mankind, and grounds blessedness on the relationship of sonship to God, as well as on the Kingdom of God. [104]

According to Ritschl, the Christian religion is based on the life of Jesus as a sort of ethical redeemer and based upon him as the founder of the Kingdom of God. It also consists in fi ve things: freedom of the children of God, presumably from—as we have already seen—the world and

---

[104] Ritschl, *Justification and Reconciliation*, 13.

web of sin through an ethical elevation and lordship; the compulsion and encouragement to act out of love; the aim of creating ethical boundaries for moral organization; blessedness in one's sonship and daughtership to God by attaining the Kingdom of God through right living and ethical practice. This definition fits within the three paths of examination for both Ritschl and McLaren.

First, the problem with humanity is not the nature of individuals themselves, but our bad actions. Both McLaren and Ritschl reject the historic doctrine of original sin, rejecting the transmission of both personal guilt and divine wrath and the individual necessity to sin by nature. Instead, both agree that the systems and stories of the world are to blame for the evolving human condition. While the first parents began innocently enough and were created with the capacity to freely choose the highest common good, their evolution brought them to higher planes of moral consciousness, contributing to alienating acts. Now humans are caught: in the words of Ritschl we are caught in a whole web of sinful actions and reactions; in the words of McLaren we are caught in an avalanche of crises that are the result of dysfunctional systems and destructive stories. Both presuppose a collective "selfish bias" conscious that is the result of external bad systems and stories in the world impinging upon the individual and collective humanity. This web of systems and stories have coagulated to form a power of united sin that falls upon every person, moving us to act badly. The problem, then, is outside of us, and for that we need a better ethical system and a better story.

McLaren and Ritschl both believe the solution to our problem is found in the alternative system and story of the

Kingdom of God, which represents the highest, perfect ethical common good after which all of humanity is supposed to strive. Both also believe that one human was sent and commissioned by God as a conduit for this solution: Jesus Christ. Both Ritschl and McLaren believe the inherent value in the person and work of Jesus Christ is how He lived. Because the problem of humanity is bad actions, the means by which that problem can be solved must provide a model for better actions. Th us, they envision the person of Jesus as the prototype for the best possible way to live as a human; Jesus was a master of life and lived it in such a way that teaches all the world how to live. While they do not believe Jesus was God Himself, they both maintain that His possession of the Godhead attribute is the result of His ethical service and actions; Jesus's ethics were Divine and He revealed the character of God. Th us, He was full of God because of His loving, high righteous ethics, humanity can fi nd salvation from the bad systems and stories of the world.

There is a sort of yin-yang relationship in their theology between the person and works of Jesus: Because Jesus is full of God and sent by God to found the Kingdom, we fi nd in His life and teachings the highest, perfect common moral good; because He loved in the face of hatred and suffered in the face of imperial abuse, Jesus shows and reveals the character of the living God and He Himself participates in the Godhead. Jesus shares in the fellowship of the Divine because He is ethical; Jesus is ethical because He was in some real way chosen by God and possessed a strong connection to the Divine. Because of this connection and because of His higher divine consciousness He belongs to a higher order of human existence. We should note here how similar this belief is to the early church heresy known as adoptionism. Like this heresy, McLaren and Ritschl seem to believe that Jesus was "adopted" by God to be the Christ because of His higher Consciousness and obedience. Out of this connection, consciousness, and order, Jesus has enabled humanity to find salvation, primarily in attaining the Kingdom of God which He Himself founded and taught. As a chosen conduit who had a unique relationship with God and one who participated in the Divine through founding, teaching, and living the highest ethical common good of the Kingdom, he shows the way and leads the way of liberation from the bad systems and stories of the world. This display and liberation culminated at the cross, the ultimate showdown between the contrary ways of Kingdom of the World and Kingdom of God.

While the historic Christian faith has pointed to the cross as the means by which people find salvation from the problem of natural, inherited sin because of the substitutionary role of Jesus' sacrifice, Ritschl and McLaren imagine the cross plays a different role. For them, the cross is part of our salvation from the systems and stories of the world because of Jesus' moral example of vulnerability, suffering, and love. Again, because our human problem is an existential one, resulting from bad systems and stories, the ultimate solution must relate to a better way of living. At the cross, Jesus shows God's forgiving, rather than revenging, heart toward humanity. The cross is the window through which we see God rejecting the violence and dominance and oppression of the world over against the way of sacrifice and suffering of the Kingdom. In turn, Jesus' example of death beckons humanity to die to the systems and stories of the world and the selfish bias that results from the web of those systems, while rising with Him above those systems in loving, sacrificial triumph. By following after Jesus' ethical example on the cross, we find salvation from our bad actions.

In the end, Ritschl and McLaren believe our salvation is ultimately found in the teachings of Jesus on the Kingdom of God. The Kingdom offers the solution to the problem that has plagued humanity, because it provides dominion over the world and provides an alternative system and story. Ritschl explicitly says the solution to the problem that has confounded humans for millennia is found in the Kingdom of God precisely because it offers an ethical ordering, dominion and rallying point over against the web of sin and sin of society that defines the world. And those who have committed themselves to this new ethical system and story are called to bring it into existence in order to solve our ethical problem and find ethical salvation. It is when one orients his life around the loving action of the Kingdom and cooperates with God's Kingdom that one enters into communion with Him and is relieved of a guilty conscience. The salvation of the world and individuals is dependent upon humans actively bringing in the Kingdom through good deeds, which is why McLaren urges people of any faith and background to start doing good now and never give up until God's Kingdom dream is realized, until Jesus' alternative ethical system and story replaces those of the world.

Though this examination is not exhaustive, it should be clear that Brian McLaren's own theology mirrors, and perhaps borrows from, the theology of Albrect Ritschl. In regards to the problem, McLaren follows in the footsteps of Ritschl by rejecting original, individual inherited sin in favor of the collective conscious of the world. Th is collective conscious has developed and grown into a web of sin and power all its own, which rests on every individual. Individuals do not sin by nature, but because of the dysfunctional systems and destructive stories of the world. McLaren agrees with Ritschl that our problem is ethical. Hence, our solution and its bearer must also be ethical. Jesus Christ is envisioned by both theologians as a superman of sorts, a divinely appointed and endowed messenger sent by God to found the Kingdom, teach its alternative system and story, and live an archetypal life of righteous ethics. McLaren agrees with Ritschl that Jesus is not Himself God, but shares in His divinity and bears the attribute of the Godhead because he lived he "highest common good." In words that mirror Ritschl, McLaren says that Jesus was the highest and deepest revelation of the character of God. It is this character that saves humanity, because it provides an alternative system and story in the teachings and life of the Kingdom. McLaren clearly shares in Ritschl's soteriology by exalting the Kingdom of God as the solution to our ethical dilemma. Though the traditional Christian faith has called us to place our faith in Christ, McLaren joins Ritschl in calling people to place their faith in the Kingdom of God, for in its ethics lies our hope for salvation.

Reimagining the Christian Faith

In his new theological treatise, McLaren maintains that he is offering hope and guidance for fellow sojourners through what he has often called theological terra nova. He believes that he and others are forging a new way through new territory through Christianity by offering fresh theological perspectives for the Church. This examination reveals, however, that his new way of believing and new kind of Christianity is recycled Ritschlianism. His definition of the human problem, offered solution, and description of the solutions bearer is nothing new. Instead, it is apparent that McLaren has repackaged liberal Christian theology and is now offering it to the masses as fresh, innovative, and alternative to what Christianity has been traditionally. This is simply not the case. Roger Olson maintains that "the story of Christian theology is the story of Christian reflection on salvation." [105] This examination makes plain that the reflection on the nature of salvation offered by the emerging church and its leaders at this junction in the story is repetitive and cyclical; rehashed theological liberalism is being paraded as newfangled Christianity. It's time McLaren comes clean and acknowledge that he is a contemporary theological liberal who is refashioning contemporary Christianity in the tradition of Ritschl. Perhaps then a proper, honest dialogue can commence between him and others regarding his very old kind of Christianity and its diametrical opposition to the historic Christian faith.

---

[105] Olson, *Christian Theology*, 13.

BIBLIOGRAPHY

Livingston, James C. Modern Christian Thought: From the Enlightenment to Vatican II. New York: Macmillian, 1971.

McLaren, Brian. Th e Story We Find Ourselves In. San Francisco: Jossey-Bass, 2003.

_____. Th e Secret Message of Jesus. Nashville: Word Publishing, 2006.

_____. Everything Must Change. Nashville: Thomas Nelson Publishers, 2007.

_____. A New Kind of Christianity. New York: HarperOne, 2010.

Olson, Roger. Th e Story of Christian Th eology. Downers Grove: IVP Academic, 1999.

Ritschl, Albrecht. Instruction In Th e Christian Religion. London: Longmans, Green, and Co., 1901.

_____. The Christian Doctrine of Justification and Reconciliation. Edinburgh: T & T Clark, 1902.

Swing, Albert Temple. Th e Th eology of Albrecht Ritschl. London: Longmans, Green, and Co., 1901.

Reimagining the Christian Faith

AFTERWORD

When I try to describe and explain the theological quagmire modern evangelicalism is thanks to the Emergent Church movement, often I like to retell the story from 2 Kings 23 about young King Josiah and the High Priest Hilkiah.

This story from the Hebrew Scriptures about a lost book, a very important lost book, actually. Th is very important lost book was the foundation to Israel's life with God. And it lay missing. Forgotten, forsaken. For two generations. Like some old photo album stuffed away in Grandma's musty old attic.

While this very important lost book lay missing, a number of kings ascended the throne who introduced pagan worship practices into the life of Israel—including astrological worship, idolatry, and even child sacrifice. The people forsook their one true love—YHWH, the God of Israel—for fake gods and fake stories.

Israel lost the plot to her story as much as she lost a very important book. And it wasn't until the reign of a child king that Israel found what she had lost. During the reign of King Josiah, Israel recovered the plot to her story. Literally.

One day our very important lost book was discovered during temple renovations by one of the priests. It wasn't until it was recovered that Israel re-discovered the plot to her story and returned to worshiping and believing in the one true God.

In many ways the same is happening in the Church. No we are not worshipping pagan gods or incorporating pagan worship practices into our Sunday worship. We are losing the plot to our own story, though, because we are forgetting and forsaking God's Story.

This forgetting and forsaking isn't anything new; we've seen this before. Unfortunately, many thinkers within the Emergent Church movement are following in the same forgetting-forsaking footsteps as plenty of other thinkers before them. As we have seen from these essays, there really is "nothing new under the sun."

Emergents such as those in these essays are reimagining the major "pieces" to the Christian faith to such an extent that they've "given up the farm," so to speak. For them, God Himself has not shown Himself, and instead our language about God is merely human conjecture; sin is not my problem because I am not the problem—my environment around me and what happens to me is the problem; Jesus is viewed as a great moral teacher on the same level with Gandhi; and, in the end, everyone wins because love wins.

Like Israel, the Church needs to recover the plot to our Story. And I hope my generation takes the lead in retracing the steps of those who've gone before us in order to rediscover what the Church has always believed about God, creation, humanity, sin, Jesus Christ, faith, and salvation.

Leave it up to a child to lead Israel to repentance and back into rightly believing in and behaving with God. And leave it up to the next generation, my generation, to lead the Church back to the fundamentals of God's Story of Rescue by rediscovering the historic Christian faith.

Reimagining the Christian Faith

FIVE GENERATIONS OF LIBERAL KINGDOM GRAMMAR

If you liked this short book, you would probably like a larger book that examines several key features of Emergent theology alongside four prominent historic theological liberal voices. You may purchase *Reimagining the Kingdom* in print at most online retailers. You may also purchase an ebook for NOOK and Kindle.

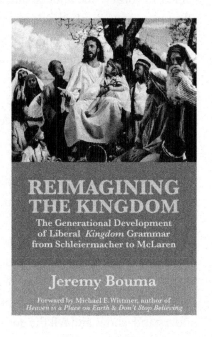

In recent years the use of Kingdom of God language has markedly increased within evangelicalism, and rightly so, as the Kingdom is central to the teachings of Jesus. While recapturing this aspect of the Christian faith is a good thing, several scholars have noted similarities between such language and Protestant liberalism. Th ese scholars, however, have not significantly explored these similarities or the impact liberal Kingdom grammar is having on evangelical notions of the Kingdom.

Reimagining the Kingdom traces the development of Kingdom grammar through four generations of liberalism-from Schleiermacher to Ritschl, Rauschenbusch, and Tillich-in order to understand how such grammar is affecting evangelical theology, particularly the variety espoused by so-called "Emergent" progressive evangelicals. By exploring how theological liberals define the human problem, understand that problem's solution, and interpret the nature of the One who bore that solution, this book reveals an inextricable link between progressive Emergent evangelicalism and Protestant liberalism.

As with liberal Kingdom grammar, progressive evangelicals ultimately urge people to place their faith in the way of Jesus-i.e. the Kingdom of God- rather than the person and work of Jesus. Th is is a significant departure from authentic, historic Christianity. Therefore, it is imperative that evangelicals understand the contours of liberal Kingdom grammar in order to understand how such grammar is affecting how some evangelicals understand, show, and tell the gospel itself.